You are
a joy to
work with!
May God be your
guide always

Veretta

150 Days of Praise

VENETIA FROST

www.venetiafrost.com

WESTBOW·
PRESS
A DIVISION OF THOMAS NELSON
& ZONDERVAN

WestBow Press books may be ordered through booksellers or by contacting:

WestBow Press
A Division of Thomas Nelson & Zondervan
1663 Liberty Drive
Bloomington, IN 47403
www.westbowpress.com
1 (866) 928-1240

ISBN: 978-1-4908-4413-8 (sc)
ISBN: 978-1-4908-4414-5 (e)

Library of Congress Control Number: 2014912237

Printed in the United States of America.

WestBow Press rev. date: 09/05/2014

PREFACE

Everyone has had times in his life when things seemed to overwhelm him. But knowing you have a God who is greater than any trial you will encounter gives you the faith to face every day. There was a time in my life when it seemed like a thick cloud of darkness hung over me. Although I had many good things in my life to be thankful for, it seemed like my heart just had no joy. I felt like there was no hope of escape. Can you relate? But I learned the power of praising God through this Praise Devotional. I began having victory in circumstances in my life. With each victory, I gained more and more confidence in God's Love for me and His Faithfulness to me. And the thick cloud of darkness hanging over me has vanished! I now have real joy; and a confidence that every foe of mine will fall before the God who lives in me and walks beside me. Life is positively thrilling now!

A second and also very important thing God taught me through this Praise Devotional is the power of speaking the Word aloud. For years I just read the Word of God silently to myself. I loved God, but I had little victory or joy in my life. As I learned to speak God's Word aloud, I found not only did my faith in God arise; but my enemies fell before the Word of the Lord! Whenever a need or circumstance came against me, I found a scripture that answered the problem. I prayed that scripture aloud. My faith in God was there because of the intimacy produced throughout this Praise Devotional. So in faith I spoke His Word aloud and Satan had no choice but to flee!

In 2 Chronicles 20: 21-23 Jehoshaphat sent his singers in front of the army because he bowed his face before the Lord and God said "this battle is not ours but it belongs to the Lord". The enemies of the children of God were utterly destroyed by their own hand because the children of God obeyed and sang praises to Him.

The *150 Days of Praise Devotional* is instrumental in destroying the enemy who comes against us with depression and life's struggles. By reading the Psalms (God's blue print for Praise-His word), writing it out and speaking the Psalm and word of God through the day; it enables us to overcome depression, and self- defeating thoughts. Then we can walk in the victory God has already accomplished through His Son "Jesus". And we can fulfill the plan He has for our life.

Michael J. Frost CEO. Life of Christ Ministries Inc.

I was given the opportunity to do the 150 Days of Praise in the fall of 2012. I am thankful that it was put in my heart to pray before reading each day and that I was able to finish the 150 Days of Praise and I now have a better understanding of God's Word. I have every intention of repeating the 150 Days of Praise, it helped so much in my understanding that God is forever by my side and with me every step of the way.

Liz Winfield

ACKNOWLEDGEMENT

I would so like to thank my husband first for his belief in me. Also great thanks to my pastor's wife, Jelly Valimont (Jelly Valimont is author of *I Have Issues* which can be found at: Amazon.com; RandyValimont.com; or griffinfirst.org); of Griffin First Assembly, Griffin, Georgia. Their support, input and encouragement helped me to know that this was a call from God. Jelly Valimont also edited the book, pulling me to greater heights of writing.

INTRODUCTION

My dear one, are you tired of the darkness that attacks your heart? Do you dream of happy days? Do you want the power to live that good and joyous life? You can have them. This devotional was prepared just for you. God has created a way for us to take advantage of His power; and defeat the things that beforehand have overwhelmed us. <u>God wants you to have a good life!</u> The key to having that good life is having joy in your heart. Joy comes only from intimacy with God. Intimacy is really such a beautiful word. It speaks of a closeness and love that is just between the two of you. It speaks of sweet times and trust in Him. God is not some far away, mysterious deity that you are supposed to believe in without any personal experience and relationship. God longs for an intimate relationship with you. And intimacy with God gives you joy. This devotional develops your intimacy with God. As your intimacy with God develops, His Glory fills you. As His Glory fills you, He drives out fear, insecurities, and pain (wounds) of your soul. So, as intimacy increases, so does victory in every situation in life. Any dark forces evil may offer, God's Presence will drive out. So the real question is: do you want to keep the darkness and depression; or do you want peace and wholeness, joy and victory?

Do you know the story in Joshua chapter 6 in the Bible where Joshua and the Israelites marched around the city of Jericho for 6 days? Following God's orders, on the 7th day they marched 7 times; then they shouted and the walls fell down. The Israelites went in and conquered their enemy! Learning to speak the Word of God aloud is essential to living the victorious life Christ died to give you. We have used our mouths long enough to allow Satan access into our lives.

It is time we (as the people of God) stood up as Joshua and the Israelites did and praise a holy God; bringing down the obstacles in our life with the Word of God. While gossiping and complaining attracts evil spirits, praise and faith in the Word of God actually attracts the Presence of God! There is nothing more dangerous to Satan than someone: who walks in love and forgiveness; who loves, believes and obeys God; who prays – not only for others, but keeps an intimate fellowship/relationship with God through prayer; and who speaks the Word of God aloud into their circumstances. There is so much power in believing God; in speaking His Word aloud; and in living in a love relationship with God that you become an unmovable, unstoppable and an unbeatable force! This is what God wants in your life – not defeat. The reason great men and women of the bible (and in these days) are so victorious (not only in their own life but also in impacting others for Christ); is because of their <u>intimacy with God</u>. Their life is a result of being filled with the Glory and the Presence of God! You just don't get faith in God without intimacy with Him.

Each day as you read, write and speak out loud you will find your hope and faith arising. Joy will also come. Do not let Satan steal what God has for you. The Word becomes activated in your life as you believe it and speak it out loud. I just cannot say enough how important praise is to every Christian. It brings reverence for God (a seriously lost concept these days); intimacy with God; and victory in all of life's circumstances as your faith arises and takes hold of God's promises.

On each page of this devotional you will find that I have used the last three stages of a butterfly to identify our stages of spiritual growth each day. The first stage (which I did not use) is the egg. The egg represents your birth (spiritual re-birth); that is being born again. The three stages we will use are as follows: the first stage (which is the caterpillar) is where we ingest (read) the Word. A caterpillar is said to eat and eat and eat in order to prepare itself for the pupa stage. To me, the caterpillar up close is a very unattractive creature. But without God changing us, so are we in our hearts. The second stage is the pupa stage. This is when the caterpillar wraps itself up inside a cocoon and hibernates until it is recreated into a completely different likeness. With the Word of God inside of us, we allow it to do its work in us. The bible teaches us we are to be made in Christ's likeness. The adult stage is to me the most beautiful because it is the result of all the eating and meditating. When we come out of our metamorphosis, we too will be changed into someone beautiful inside! There is reading, writing and speaking to do every day. There is room on the bottom or back of each page for you to write.

I pray you will find this devotional life-changing for you as it was for me as God took me through it!

DAY 1

<u>Stage 1: Caterpillar</u> (remember he devours much food in preparation) First, read the Scripture to yourself.

Psalms 1:1-3

"Blessed is the man who will not take advice of the ungodly nor act like or talk like them. 2) But his delight is in the law (the Words) of the Lord; and <u>in His Words does that man meditate day & night</u>. 3) And that man shall be as a tree which is planted by the rivers of water. He will bring forth his fruit in due season. His leaf will not wither. <u>And whatever he does will prosper</u>!"

<u>Stage 2: Pupa</u> (he goes into a state of seclusion) So you will **rewrite the Scripture in your own handwriting.** Then meditate a few minutes on the meaning of these wonderful scriptures. This is important to help get the Word into your heart.

<u>Stage 3: Butterfly</u> (Maturity comes about as you <u>let the Word work in you.</u>) **Read, pray, or sing these verses out loud two or three times to God.** This is a very important stage for in doing this every day you will begin to grow in strength. Before you know it, your life will start changing and the hard times will be under your feet! Victory is yours. So do not let anything hinder you from this every day until the time is finished! Let this be your focus today: take the Scripture that speaks the most to you today and speak it all day long.

Journal notes:

DAY 2

Stage 1: Caterpillar (remember he devours much food in preparation) First, read the Scripture to yourself.

Psalms 2: 7-8,12b

"I will declare the decree (for) the Lord has said unto me; You are My child, this day have I begotten you. 8) Ask of Me, and I shall give you the heathen as your inheritance (for a servant); and (I will give you) the uttermost parts of the earth for your possession. 12)...blessed are they who will put their trust in Me."

Stage 2: Pupa (he goes into a state of seclusion) So you will **rewrite the Scripture in your own handwriting.** Then meditate a few minutes on the meaning of these wonderful scriptures. This is important to help get the Word into your heart.

Stage 3: Butterfly (Maturity comes about as you let the Word work in you.) **Read, pray, or sing these verses out loud two or three times to God.** This is a very important stage for in doing this every day you will begin to grow in strength. Before you know it, your life will start changing and the hard times will be under your feet! Victory is yours. So do not let anything hinder you from this every day until the time is finished! Today thank God that He has said these things over you personally.

Journal notes:

DAY 3

<u>Stage 1: Caterpillar</u> (remember he devours much food in preparation) First, read the Scripture to yourself.

Psalms 3:3

"But thou, O Lord, are a shield for me; my glory and the lifter of my head."

<u>Stage 2: Pupa</u> (he goes into a state of seclusion) So you will **rewrite the Scripture in your own handwriting.** Then meditate a few minutes on the meaning of these wonderful scriptures. This is important to help get the Word into your heart.

<u>Stage 3: Butterfly</u> (Maturity comes about as you <u>let the Word work in you.</u>) **Read, pray, or sing these verses out loud two or three times to God.** This one you will sing out loud all day long as you <u>envision God as a shield around you.</u>

Journal notes:

DAY 4

Stage 1: Caterpillar (remember he devours much food in preparation) First, read the Scripture to yourself.

Psalms 4:3-8 "But <u>know</u> that the Lord has set apart he who is godly unto Himself. The Lord will hear when you call unto Him. 4) Stand in awe of God and sin not. 5) Put your trust in the Lord. 6) Lord, lift up the light of Your Countenance (Face) upon us. 7) For You have put gladness in my heart. 8) I will both lay me down in peace, and sleep; for You alone, O Lord, make me to dwell in safety."

Psalms 5:11-12 "Let all those who put their trust in You rejoice. Let us forever shout for joy, because You defend us (and You are on our side). Let us also that love Your Name be joyful in You. 12) For You, O Lord, will bless the righteous. With favor you will surround me as with a shield."

Stage 2: Pupa (he goes into a state of seclusion) So you will **rewrite the Scripture in your own handwriting.** Then meditate a few minutes on the meaning of these wonderful scriptures. This is important to help get the Word into your heart.

Stage 3: Butterfly (Maturity comes about as you <u>let the Word work in you.</u>) **Read, pray, or sing these verses out loud two or three times to God.** Peace and joy are to be your companions during the day; and you should sleep knowing God is your protector. Today's Scriptures also tell us to s-h-o-u-t! It says to be joyful in God. Then it tells us that He will surround us with favor like a shield. Go today expecting favor!

Journal notes:

DAY 5

<u>Stage 1: Caterpillar</u> (remember he devours much food in preparation) First, read the Scripture to yourself.

Psalms 6:8-10 "Depart from me, all ye workers of iniquity; for <u>the Lord has heard the voice of my weeping.</u> 9) The Lord has heard my supplications. The Lord will receive my prayer. 10) Let all my enemies be ashamed and sore vexed. Let them depart from me and be shown for what they are immediately."

Psalms 7:1, 1 7 "O Lord my God, in You do I put my trust. For You save me from my enemy and You deliver me. 17) I will praise You Lord because of Your righteousness; and I will sing praises to the Name of the Lord, the most High God!"

<u>Stage 2: Pupa</u> (he goes into a state of seclusion) So you will **rewrite the Scripture in your own handwriting.** Then meditate a few minutes on the meaning of these wonderful scriptures. This is important to help get the Word into your heart.

<u>Stage 3: Butterfly</u> (Maturity comes about as you <u>let the Word work in you.</u>) **Read, pray, or sing these verses out loud to God.** As you do, affirm that God is on your side. The Lord is your defense. Today, declare that God will save you from your enemies.

Journal notes:

DAY 6

Stage 1: Caterpillar (remember he devours much food in preparation) First, read the Scripture to yourself.

Psalms 8:1-3, 5-6, 9 "O Lord, our Lord, how excellent/majestic is Your Name in all the earth. 2) Out of the mouth of babes and suck lings You have ordained strength... that You might shut up/stop the enemy. 3) When I consider the heavens, the work of Your fingers. 5) You have crowned man with glory and honor. 6) You have given him dominion over all the work of Your hands. You have put all things under man's feet. 9) O Lord, our Lord, how excellent/majestic is Your Name in all the earth."

Stage 2: Pupa (he goes into a state of seclusion) So you will **rewrite the Scripture in your own handwriting.** Then meditate a few minutes on the meaning of these wonderful scriptures. This is important to help get the Word into your heart.

Stage 3: Butterfly (Maturity comes about as you <u>let the Word work in you.</u>) **Read, pray, or sing these verses out loud to God.** Sing these verses over and over out loud to the Lord, praising Him for His beauty. Let this be your focus today: take the Scripture that speaks the most to you today and speak it all day long.

Journal notes:

DAY 7

<u>Stage 1: Caterpillar</u> (remember he devours much food in preparation) First, read the Scripture to yourself.

Psalms 9:1-5, 8-14 "I will praise You, O Lord, with my whole heart. I will speak of and praise You for all Your marvelous works. 2) I will be glad and rejoice in You. I will sing praise to Your Name, O thou most High. 3) My enemies shall fall and perish at Your Presence. 4) You maintained my cause; You judge righteously. 5) You have rebuked the heathen and destroyed the wicked... 8) The Lord shall minister justice. 9) The Lord will be a refuge for the oppressed; a refuge in times of trouble. 10) They who know Your Name will put their trust in You; for You, Lord have never forsaken those who seek You. 11) (I) sing praises to the Lord and I declare His works. 12) (God) forgets not the cry of the humble. 13) Lift me up 14) that I may show forth all Your praise. I will rejoice in Your salvation."

<u>Stage 2: Pupa</u> (he goes into a state of seclusion) So you will **rewrite the Scripture in your own handwriting.** Then meditate a few minutes on the meaning of these wonderful scriptures. This is important to help get the Word into your heart.

<u>Stage 3: Butterfly</u> (Maturity comes about as you <u>let the Word work in you.</u>) **Read, pray, or sing these verses out loud two or three times to God.** Let this be your focus today: take the Scripture that speaks the most to you today and speak it all day long.

Journal notes:

DAY 8

<u>Stage 1: Caterpillar</u> (remember he devours much food in preparation) First, read the Scripture to yourself.

Psalms 10:12, 16-18 "Arise, O Lord, O God, lift up Your Hand; forget not the humble. 16) The Lord is King forever and ever. 17) Lord, You hear the needs, cries and desires of the humble. You will prepare their heart. Your ear hears their call. 18) You bring justice to the fatherless and the oppressed that they may be oppressed no more!"

Psalms 11:1 "In You, O Lord, I will put my trust."

<u>Stage 2: Pupa</u> (he goes into a state of seclusion) So you will **rewrite the Scripture in your own handwriting.** Then meditate a few minutes on the meaning of these wonderful scriptures. This is important to help get the Word into your heart.

<u>Stage 3: Butterfly</u> (Maturity comes about as you <u>let the Word work in you.</u>) **Read, pray, or sing these verses out loud two or three times to God.** Then sing these verses over and over out loud to the Lord all day long; praising Him for His faithfulness.

Journal notes:

DAY 9

<u>Stage 1: Caterpillar</u> (remember he devours much food in preparation) First, read the Scripture to yourself.

Psalms 12:3, 5-7 "The Lord will cut off (in this land) all flattering (lying) lips and the tongue that boasts. 5) <u>For the oppression of the poor, for the cry of the needy, now will I arise, saith the Lord.</u> I will set you in safety from the one attacking you. 6) The words of the Lord are pure words; as silver tried (purified) in an earthen furnace, purified 7 times. 7) You shall keep them O Lord; You will preserve Your children from the evil ones forever."

13:5-6 "I have trusted in Your mercy. My heart shall rejoice in Your salvation. 6) I will sing unto the Lord because He has dealt bountifully with me!"

<u>Stage 2: Pupa</u> (he goes into a state of seclusion) So you will **rewrite the Scripture in your own handwriting.** Then meditate a few minutes on the meaning of these wonderful scriptures. This is important to help get the Word into your heart.

<u>Stage 3: Butterfly</u> (Maturity comes about as you <u>let the Word work in you.</u>) Sing these scriptures to the Lord, thanking Him for defending you. Remember today that verse 5 of both chapters says God will arise to defend you. You can trust in His mercy and rejoice in His salvation. Declare that out loud all day.

Journal notes:

DAY 10

Stage 1: Caterpillar (remember he devours much food in preparation) First, read the Scripture to yourself.

Psalms 14: 5-7 "...God is with the generation of the righteous. 6) The Lord is the refuge of the poor. 7) O that the salvation of Israel were come out of Zion! The Lord is freeing His people and releasing them from captivity. And there shall be great rejoicing; for the Lord is our deliverer!"

Stage 2: Pupa (he goes into a state of seclusion) So you will **rewrite the Scripture in your own handwriting.** Then meditate a few minutes on the meaning of these wonderful scriptures. This is important to help get the Word into your heart.

Stage 3: Butterfly (Maturity comes about as you <u>let the Word work in you.</u>) **Pray this scripture out loud to God over and over.** Meditate a few minutes on the meaning of this wonderful promise from God for He is speaking this to you. Sing verse 6 all day saying continually: The Lord is my refuge and deliverer!

Journal notes:

DAY 11

Stage 1: Caterpillar (remember he devours much food in preparation) First, read the Scripture to yourself.

Psalms 15: 1-5 "Lord who shall abide in Your tabernacle or dwell in Your holy hill? 2) Only he who walks upright; works righteousness; speaks the truth in his heart; 3) he that will not back bite with his tongue; who will do no evil to his neighbor; 4) one who hates evil workers but honors those who fear/revere the Lord; one who will stand by his word; 5) one who does not try to cheat nor is greedy at the expense of the poor and one who will protect the innocent. For this man shall never be moved or removed."

Stage 2: Pupa (he goes into a state of seclusion) So you will **rewrite the Scripture in your own handwriting.** Then meditate a few minutes on the meaning of these wonderful scriptures. This is important to help get the Word into your heart.

Stage 3: Butterfly (Maturity comes about as you let the Word work in you.) Pray this scripture out loud to God 2 or 3 times. Meditate a few minutes on the meaning of integrity of our heart. A person who is honorable will receive more protection from God in times that others will not. Honor in your behavior is an old idea, but not old-fashioned. Ask God to help you become as He wants you want to be. Let this be your focus today: take the Scripture that speaks the most to you today and speak it all day long.

Journal notes:

DAY 12

Stage 1: Caterpillar (remember he devours much food in preparation) First, read the Scripture to yourself.

Psalms 16: 1-3, 5-9, 11 "Preserve me, O God, in You I place my trust, 2) My soul says to the Lord You are my Lord. 3) The saints in the earth are His delight. 5) The Lord is my inheritance. You maintain my lot (of inheritance). 6) The lines have fallen to me in pleasant places. Yes, I have a goodly inheritance (from the Lord). 7) I will bless You Lord for You have given me wisdom, knowledge and understanding. You instruct my heart, even in the night. 8) I set You Lord always before my face. And because You are at my right hand, I shall not be moved. 9) Therefore my heart is glad; and my glory rejoices. My flesh will rest in Your hope. 11) You show me the path of life. In Your Presence there is fullness of joy. At Your Right Hand there are pleasures (good things for me) for evermore."

Stage 2: Pupa (he goes into a state of seclusion) So you will **rewrite the Scripture in your own handwriting.** Then meditate a few minutes on the meaning of these wonderful scriptures. This is important to help get the Word into your heart.

Stage 3: Butterfly (Maturity comes about as you let the Word work in you.) **Read, pray, or sing these verses out loud two or three times to God.** Today the one that speaks the most to you, take it with you and **speak it all day long**. Remind yourself all day that you have a good inheritance in God!

Journal notes:

DAY 13

<u>Stage 1: Caterpillar</u> (remember he devours much food in preparation) First, read the Scripture to yourself.

Psalms 17: 3-8, 13, 15 "...I have purposed (determined) that my mouth shall not sin (even though my enemy is pressing hard on me). 4) By Your Words I have been kept from the paths of destruction. 5) You hold me so I do not slip. 6) I have called on You and You hear. 7) Show Your marvelous loving kindness. You save with Your right hand all who will place their trust in You. You save me from my enemy that rises up against me. 8) You keep me as the apple of Your eye; and You protect me under the shadow of Your wings. 13) Arise, O Lord, and cast down my enemy! 15) I will behold Your Face in righteousness. I will be fulfilled and satisfied for You remake me into Your image-inside and out!"

<u>Stage 2: Pupa</u> (he goes into a state of seclusion) So you will **rewrite the Scripture in your own handwriting.** Then meditate a few minutes on the meaning of these wonderful scriptures. This is important to help get the Word into your heart.

<u>Stage 3: Butterfly</u> (Maturity comes about as you <u>let the Word work in you.</u>) **Read, pray, or sing these verses out loud two or three times to God.** Meditate a few minutes on the faithfulness of God. Choose one of the verses above to quote to yourself all day today as you <u>think about His faithfulness.</u>

Journal notes:

DAY 14

Stage 1: Caterpillar (remember he devours much food in preparation) First, read the Scripture to yourself.

Psalms 18: 1-3, 6-10, 13-19 "I love You, O Lord, for You are my strength. 2) You are my rock, my covering and my deliverer. You are my God, my strength and the One in whom I will trust. 3) I will call upon You Lord; You are worthy to be praised. So shall I be saved from my enemies. 6) In my trouble I called upon the Lord. I cried out unto You God; and You heard my voice in Your holy temple. My cry came up before Your ears. 7) Then the earth shook and trembled. The very hills crumbled because You were angry at my enemy. 8) Smoke and fire coming from You lit up the earth. 9) <u>You arose from Your throne.</u> You bowed the heavens and came down in my defense! 10) You flew from heaven to me. 13) Your voice thundered in the heavens. 14) You sent out arrows and scattered my enemy. You shot out lightning and put them in fear. 15) The earth broke open exposing the very foundations of the waters of the earth. 16) You sent from above and drew me out of many dangers. 17) You delivered me from the enemy that hated me; for they were stronger than me. 18) They tried to oppress me in the day of my calamity; but You Lord were my sustainer. 19) You brought me out in a larger place. You delivered me because of Your love for me."

Stage 2: Pupa (he goes into a state of seclusion) So you will **rewrite the Scripture in your own handwriting.** Then meditate a few minutes on the meaning of these wonderful scriptures. This is important to help get the Word into your heart.

Stage 3: Butterfly (Maturity comes about as you <u>let the Word work in you.</u>) **Declare out loud these verses to God with vigor.** As you do, know <u>God is</u> what they say. As we read today's, we turned all 'He' into 'You, God' to personalize what God does for you. Often as I read the scriptures to myself out loud, I change He into You, God. You may not have known this, but God gets very angry when you are messed with, for <u>you are His child.</u> Depend on

Him for your defense. These verses are an amazing picture of how the earth shakes when God arises to defend you. Meditate today on God's defense of you. When the enemy thinks you are defeated, God will turn it around and bring you into greater blessings than you had before they messed with you <u>because you place your trust in Him.</u> Sing verse 3 all day.

Journal notes:

DAY 15

Stage 1: Caterpillar (remember he devours much food in preparation) First, read the Scripture to yourself.

Psalms 18: 20-27, 29-39 "The Lord rewarded me according to my faithfulness and innocence in this matter. <u>The Lord will recompense me everything taken by my enemy.</u> 21) For I have kept His commandments; and I have not left my God. 22) I kept all Your judgments before my eyes; and I forgot none of Your commandments to me. 23) I kept myself innocent in this matter. 24) Therefore the Lord has been able to recompense me. 25) To the merciful man You give mercy. To the righteous man You cover him with righteousness. 26) To the pure hearted You show favor and goodness. To the evil, You reward him with evil. 27) You save those who are oppressed; and You bring to nothing those who are high and mighty with pride. 29) You have given me the strength to run through a whole troop. With my God I have leaped over a wall. 30) Your way is perfect; Your Word is tried and true. You are stability to all those who trust in You. 31) For who is God; except our Lord. Who is a rock except our God! 32) It is God who girds me with His strength; and perfects my path. 33) You cause my feet to be as sure as a doe's when climbing high places. You set me upon my high places. 34) You give strength to my arms. 35) You have given me the shield of Your salvation. Your right hand upholds me; and Your gentleness has made me mighty in battle. 36) You have increased my path, so that my steps will not slip. 37) I have pursued my enemy and overtaken them. I totally wiped them out. 38) My enemy (anger, lack, sickness and despair) will never rise again; for they are fallen under my feet because of the strength You have given me. 39) You have girded me with strength for the battle; and You have subdued under me any who rose up against me."

Stage 2: Pupa (he goes into a state of seclusion) **Rewrite the Scripture in your own handwriting.** Then meditate a few minutes on the meaning of these wonderful scriptures. This is important to help get the Word into your heart.

Stage 3: Butterfly (Maturity comes about as you <u>let the Word work in you.</u>) **Read, pray, or sing these verses out loud 2 or 3 times to God.** All of chapter 18 in Psalms shows us the defeat of our enemy, no matter whom or what your enemy is. Let this really sink into your spirit that <u>God has given you the victory over everything the devil tries to bring against you!</u> You are victorious; not a victim! Think today and for several days on these verses.

Journal notes:

DAY 16

Stage 1: Caterpillar (remember he devours much food in preparation) First, read the Scripture to yourself.

Psalms 18: 40-50 "You have given me the necks of my enemies. You have given me victory over every enemy. 41) Who was there to defend them? 42) I completely wiped out the enemy. They blew away with the wind. 43) You delivered me from strife. You made me the head and not the tail (that means one in authority; not a slave type). My enemy will serve me. 44) As soon as they hear of me, they will obey me; for I speak with Your Authority. They obey me and submit themselves to me because of You in me. 45) Strangers and demons will fear. 46) The Lord lives. Blessed be my rock. Let the God of my salvation be exalted. 47) God avenges me. You raise me up into high places and subdue the enemy under me. 48) You deliver me from my enemy. You lift me up above those who come against me. You have delivered me from the violent. 49) This is why I will give praise to my God, my King. Among the heathen I will sing praises to Your Name. 50) You give great deliverance to Your kings (of which I am one); and You show mercy to Your anointed (that is me too)!"

Stage 2: Pupa (he goes into a state of seclusion) **Rewrite the Scripture in your own handwriting.** Then meditate a few minutes on the meaning of these wonderful scriptures. This is important to help get the Word into your heart.

Stage 3: Butterfly (Maturity comes about as you <u>let the Word work in you.</u>) **Read, pray, or sing these verses out loud two or three times to God.** We must get rid of our defeated way of thinking. As you can see from all of Psalms 18, we are not defeated; therefore we should not think in defeated terms. We should not speak, act or feel defeated. PRAISE GOD, using these and other scriptures <u>whenever</u> you feel the spirit of defeat trying to come on

you. Those evil spirits must leave in the presence of praise! Let this be your focus today: take the Scripture that speaks the most to you today and speak it all day long.

Journal notes:

DAY 17

Stage 1: Caterpillar (remember he devours much food in preparation) First, read the Scripture to yourself.

Psalms 19: 1-3, 7-11, 14 "The heavens declare Your Glory, O God. The firmament shows Your handiwork! 2) Day unto day speaks of You. Night after night shows Your knowledge. (How can we imagine this world came into being without a magnificent Creator?!) 3) There is nowhere where Your magnificence and Your creations are not seen by everyone alive. 7) Your law is perfect for it converts the soul of man. Your testimony is truth, sure, firm and it makes the simple man wise! 8) Your statutes are just and bring joy and rejoicing to my heart. Your commandment is pure; enlightening my understanding! 9) Reverence for You is pure and endures forever. Your judgments are truth and altogether (completely) righteous. 10) Your judgments (decisions and justice) should be sought after more than the finest and most abundant of gold; because they are more valuable than all the gold in the world. (All the gold in the world cannot compare to seeking Your wisdom for my life. Your Presence is to be chased after and desired more than anything this dying world has.) 11) By Your justice, we are warned and kept away from many dangers. There is great reward and blessing in keeping Your commandments. 14) I pray You help me keep my words, my thoughts and the motives of my heart clean, pure and holy before You. You are my strength and my redeemer. You have redeemed me and bought me from the enemy who had me in chains of mental and emotional darkness and despair. (But I am there no longer because of Your Love and mercy on me!)"

Stage 2: Pupa (he goes into a state of seclusion) **Rewrite the Scripture in your own handwriting.** Then meditate a few minutes on the meaning of these wonderful scriptures. This is important to help get the Word into your heart.

Stage 3: Butterfly (Maturity comes about as you <u>let the Word work in you.</u>) **Read, pray, or sing these verses out loud two or three times to God.** Today the one that speaks the most to you, take it with you and **speak it all day long**. Meditate a few minutes on the beauty of creation and the type of God it takes to create it. All of creation declares just how glorious and good God is! Praise Him all day today for His goodness!

Journal notes:

DAY 18

Stage 1: Caterpillar (remember he devours much food in preparation) First, read the Scripture to yourself.

Psalms 20 "The Lord hears me in the day of my calamity. The Name of the God of Jacob defends me! 2) You send me help out of Your sanctuary (Heaven) and You strengthen me out of Zion. 3) You remember all my offerings. You accept my sacrifices. 4) You grant me the desires of my heart! You fulfill the words that I speak in faith (when I believe You). 5) I rejoice in Your salvation. I set up banners In Your Name to praise Your Holy Name! The Lord answers and fulfills all my petitions (requests). 6) Now I know that the Lord saves His anointed ones (that's me). He hears from His holy heaven. And with His right hand He saves and strengthens me. 7) Some put their trust in self or money. But I will remember the Name of the Lord my God. (His Name is Almighty, All Powerful, All Holy. His Name is Love, Provider, Healer, Redeemer, Restorer of the breach!) 8) Those who trust in their own abilities will certainly fail. But we who trust in God will arise and stand upright! 9) Thank You Lord, for You hear when I call."

Stage 2: Pupa (he goes into a state of seclusion) **Rewrite the Scripture in your own handwriting.** Then meditate a few minutes on the meaning of these wonderful scriptures. This is important to help get the Word into your heart.

Stage 3: Butterfly (Maturity comes about as you let the Word work in you.) **Read, pray, or sing these verses out loud two or three times to God.** God's Name is not only holy; it is very powerful. Just calling upon His Name brings you the victory you need today! Let this be your focus today: take the Scripture that speaks the most to you today and speak it all day long.

Journal notes:

DAY 19

<u>Stage 1: Caterpillar</u> (remember he devours much food in preparation) First, read the Scripture to yourself.

Psalms 21 "I will joy in Your strength O Lord; and in Your salvation I will greatly rejoice! 2) You have given me my heart's desire and have not withheld what I have requested. 3) You surround me with good blessings. You set a crown of pure gold on my head. 4) I asked life of You and You gave it to me. 5) Glory, honor and majesty You have laid upon me. 6) You have made me most blessed forever. You have made me exceedingly happy with Your Presence. 7) For I trust in You Lord; and through Your great mercy I will never be moved (or overcome by my enemy). 8) You will route out all who hate you. 9) You will burn them up in Your anger. 10) They will be totally destroyed from off the earth. 11) Why? Because they came against me-Your beloved! They intended evil against me; which they were not able to perform. 13) We will exalt you O Lord for You are strength, beauty and majesty."

<u>Stage 2: Pupa</u> (he goes into a state of seclusion) **Rewrite the Scripture in your own handwriting.** Then meditate a few minutes on the meaning of these wonderful scriptures. This is important to help get the Word into your heart.

<u>Stage 3: Butterfly</u> (Maturity comes about as you <u>let the Word work in you.</u>) **Read, pray, or sing these verses out loud two or three times to God. You are the beloved of the Lord!** Let this be your focus today: take the Scripture that speaks the most to you today and speak it all day long.

Journal notes:

DAY 20

Stage 1: Caterpillar (remember he devours much food in preparation) First, read the Scripture to yourself.

Psalms 22: 3-5, 22-26 "You are holy. You inhabit our praises. 4) Our forefathers trusted in You and You did deliver them. 5) They cried to You and You delivered them. 22) I will declare Your Name unto all my brothers. In the midst of the congregation I will unashamedly praise You. 23) Praise the Lord, you who revere Him. Glorify and show respect unto Him. 24) For He has not despised nor rejected you in your affliction. Neither has He hid His face from you when you were in need. When you cry out to Him, He hears and answers your call. 25) Lord, my praise shall continually be of You. 26) The humble shall eat and be satisfied. They shall praise the Lord who seeks Him; and their heart shall live forever."

Stage 2: Pupa (he goes into a state of seclusion) **Rewrite the Scripture in your own handwriting.** Then meditate a few minutes on the meaning of these wonderful scriptures. This is important to help get the Word into your heart.

Stage 3: Butterfly (Maturity comes about as you let the Word work in you.) **Read, pray, or sing these verses out loud two or three times to God.** Let this be your focus today: take the Scripture that speaks the most to you today and speak it all day long.

Journal notes:

DAY 21

<u>Stage 1: Caterpillar</u> (remember he devours much food in preparation) First, read the Scripture to yourself.

Psalms 23 "Lord You are my shepherd. (Because You are) I shall not be in want or need. 2)You cause me to lie down in lush green provision where there is safety. You also lead me to the path so I may drink in peace. 3) You restore my soul (with calm and healing). You lead me in the path of righteousness for Your Name's sake (because You are a righteous God). 4) Yea, even though I may sometimes walk through the valley of the shadow of death, yet I will fear no evil. Why? It is because You God are forever by my side, with me every step of the way. Your rod and Your staff provide protection and direction for my every move. 5) You prepare a table of great abundance for me in front of my enemy so they know You are a God of love, tenderness, forgiveness, kindness and abundance. You anoint my head with oil (the Holy Spirit) so I am marked as Yours with Your holy Presence ever on me. My cup overflows with all Your goodness. 6) Surely goodness and mercy shall follow me giving me abundance of Your blessings all the days of my life. And I will dwell in the house of the Lord forever and ever."

<u>Stage 2: Pupa</u> (he goes into a state of seclusion) **Rewrite the Scripture in your own handwriting.** Then meditate a few minutes on the meaning of these wonderful scriptures. This is important to help get the Word into your heart.

<u>Stage 3: Butterfly</u> (Maturity comes about as you <u>let the Word work in you.</u>) **Read, pray, or sing these verses out loud to God.** Daily as you declare the Word of God out loud, you will find your heart expanding to make capacity for love, blessings, peace and abundance. The more we declare His Word out loud, the more He is able to move in our lives bringing freedom! Let this be your focus today: take the Scripture that speaks the most to you today and speak it all day long.

Journal notes:

DAY 22

<u>Stage 1: Caterpillar</u> (remember he devours much food in preparation) First, read the Scripture to yourself.

Psalms 24:1-8 "The earth is the Lord's, and the fullness thereof; so is the world and all who are in it. 2) For You have created the foundation of the earth and You established it. 3) Who can ascend into the Holy hill of the Lord? Who can stand in the Presence of the Lord? 4) Only that one who has clean hands and a pure heart; who has not lifted up his soul unto deceit. 5) That one shall receive the blessing from the Lord; and righteousness from God. 6) This is the generation of them who seek God; who seek the face of God. 7) Lift up your heads and the King of glory shall come in. 8) Who is this King of glory? He is the Lord strong and mighty, mighty in battle (and Glory)!"

<u>Stage 2: Pupa</u> (he goes into a state of seclusion) **Rewrite the Scripture in your own handwriting.** Then meditate a few minutes on the meaning of these wonderful scriptures. This is important to help get the Word into your heart.

<u>Stage 3: Butterfly</u> (Maturity comes about as you <u>let the Word work in you.</u>) **Read, pray, or sing these verses out loud two or three times to God.** Let this be your focus today: take the Scripture that speaks the most to you today and speak it all day long.

Journal notes:

DAY 23

Stage 1: Caterpillar (remember he devours much food in preparation) First, read the Scripture to yourself.

Psalms 25: 1-10, 13-15 "Unto You O Lord do I lift up my soul. 2) God I put my trust in You. You do not let my enemies triumph over me. 3) You let none down who wait on You. 4) Lord show me Your ways. Teach me Your paths. 5) Lead me into Your truth and teach me. You are the God of my salvation. I wait on You and in You I place my trust. 6) Never forget Your tender mercies and Your loving kindnesses; for they have always been. 7) Forget the sins of my youth. Remember me for Your goodness' sake, Lord. 8) You are good and upright; therefore You teach sinners the right way. 9) You guide the humble in justice. 10) All your paths are mercy and truth to those who keep Your covenant. 13) The man who reveres the Lord, his soul shall dwell in ease. His seed shall inherit the earth. 14) The Lord shows His covenant to that man who reveres Him. 15) My eyes always look unto You Lord. You pluck my feet out of the trap the enemy sets."

Stage 2: Pupa (he goes into a state of seclusion) **Rewrite the Scripture in your own handwriting.** Then meditate a few minutes on the meaning of these wonderful scriptures. This is important to help get the Word into your heart.

Stage 3: Butterfly (Maturity comes about as you <u>let the Word work in you.</u>) **Read, pray, or sing these verses out loud to God.** Verse 14 says the Lord shows His covenant to the man who reveres Him. God's covenant means our peace, salvation, safety, healing, provision, wisdom and abundance of blessings. What is your part? Revere God. That means: A) Recognize in your heart that He is supreme. B) Dedicate your love and allegiance to Him. C) Follow Him whole-heartedly, never looking back. Let this be your focus today: take the Scripture that speaks the most to you today and speak it all day long.

Journal notes:

DAY 24

<u>**Stage 1: Caterpillar**</u> (remember he devours much food in preparation) First, read the Scripture to yourself.

Psalms 26: 1-4, 7-8 "Know my heart O Lord. I have walked in integrity. And I have placed my trust in You for I know in doing that I cannot fail. 2) Examine my heart, motives and thoughts O God. Look deep into the innermost recesses of my soul. (I open up every part of myself for Your light to shine. I want nothing hidden from You O God). 3) Your loving kindness is ever before me. That is the light that shined so I would know how to walk in the truth. 4) I have determined in my heart not to behave as the vile do. 7) That I may speak with the voice of thanksgiving. And I will shout everywhere, telling of Your wondrous works (and Your mighty acts of goodness to Your people). 8) Lord, I love being in Your House (where Your Presence dwells)."

<u>**Stage 2: Pupa**</u> (he goes into a state of seclusion) **Rewrite the Scripture in your own handwriting.** Then meditate a few minutes on the meaning of these wonderful scriptures. This is important to help get the Word into your heart.

<u>**Stage 3: Butterfly**</u> (Maturity comes about as you <u>let the Word work in you.</u>) **Read, pray, or sing these verses out loud to God.** This chapter talks about two very important aspects of our relationship to God. Verses one and two deal with being very open to God's examining our heart and motives. Verses four and seven deals with us praising God continually with our mouth. Let this be your focus today: take the Scripture that speaks the most to you today and speak it all day long.

Journal notes:

DAY 25

Stage 1: Caterpillar (remember he devours much food in preparation) First, read the Scripture to yourself.

Psalms 27: 1-8, 13-14 "Lord, You are my light and my salvation; whom shall I fear? You are the strength of my life; of whom shall I be afraid? 2) When my enemies come upon me to devour me, they stumble and fall. 3) Even though a whole army comes against me, my heart shall not fear. Though war should rise against me, in this one thing will I be confident: 4) One thing have I desired of the Lord, that will I seek after: that I may dwell in the house (Presence) of the Lord all the days of my life, to behold the beauty of the Lord and to inquire in His temple. 5) For in the time of trouble You will hide me. 6) And now shall my head be lifted up above my enemies. Therefore I will offer sacrifices of joy. I will sing praises to the Lord. 7) You Lord hear when I cry. 8) The Lord said to me 'Seek My Face'. And I said to the Lord, Lord Your Face (beauty) I will seek and long for. 13) I would have fainted unless I had believed I would see the goodness of the Lord in the land of the living. 14) Wait on the Lord. Be of good courage and He will strengthen your heart. Wait, I say on the Lord."

Stage 2: Pupa (he goes into a state of seclusion) **Rewrite the Scripture in your own handwriting.** Then meditate a few minutes on the meaning of these wonderful scriptures. This is important to help get the Word into your heart.

Stage 3: Butterfly (Maturity comes about as you let the Word work in you.) **Read, pray, or sing these verses out loud to God two or three times.** There should be a deep hunger in our heart for the Presence of the Lord! This chapter shows us the connection between our hunger for His Presence; and His covering over us to protect us from our enemy. Let this be your focus today: take the Scripture that speaks the most to you today and speak it all day long.

Journal notes:

DAY 26

<u>Stage 1: Caterpillar</u> (remember he devours much food in preparation) First, read the Scripture to yourself.

Psalms 28: 6-7, 9 "Blessed are You Lord because You have heard my cry. 7) You are my strength and my shield. My heart trusts in You and You help me. Therefore I have great joy in my heart because I know my God saves me. I will praise You in song. 9) Save your people. Bless Your inheritance. Also feed them and lift them up forever."

Psalms 29: 1-2, 9-11 "Give unto the Lord, O ye mighty. Give unto the Lord glory, strength and praise. 2) Give unto the Lord the glory due His Name. Worship the Lord in the beauty of His Holiness. 9) In His temple does everyone speak of His glory? 10) Lord You are King forever. 11) You give strength to Your people. You will bless Your people with peace."

<u>Stage 2: Pupa</u> (he goes into a state of seclusion) **Rewrite the Scripture in your own handwriting.** Then meditate a few minutes on the meaning of these wonderful scriptures. This is important to help get the Word into your heart.

<u>Stage 3: Butterfly</u> (Maturity comes about as you <u>let the Word work in you.</u>) **Read, pray, or sing these verses out loud to God two or three times.** Whatever is bothering you today, give it to God. Trust Him to work on your behalf. That is your focus today.

Journal notes:

DAY 27

<u>Stage 1: Caterpillar</u> (remember he devours much food in preparation) First, read the Scripture to yourself.

Psalms 30: 1-2, 4-7, 11 "I will magnify You O Lord for You have lifted me up, and have not allowed my enemies to rejoice over me. 2) O Lord my God, I cried unto You and You healed me. 4) I will sing unto You Lord. I give thanks at the remembrance of Your Holiness. 5) For Your anger only endures for a moment. In Your favor there is life (for me). Weeping may endure for a night; but joy comes in the morning! 6) In my prosperity I said I shall never be moved. 7) Lord by Your favor You have made my mountain to stand strong! 11) You have turned my mourning into dancing! You have removed my mourning garments. In replacing them, You covered me with joy and gladness."

<u>Stage 2: Pupa</u> (he goes into a state of seclusion) **Rewrite the Scripture in your own handwriting.** Then meditate a few minutes on the meaning of these wonderful scriptures. This is important to help get the Word into your heart.

<u>Stage 3: Butterfly</u> (Maturity comes about as you <u>let the Word work in you.</u>) **Read, pray, or sing these verses out loud to God two or three times.** Remember today that God has removed your mourning garments. Now is the time for joy and gladness to be your covering. Shout for joy for your mourning period is over! That is your focus today.

Journal notes:

DAY 28

Stage 1: Caterpillar (remember he devours much food in preparation) First, read the Scripture to yourself.

Psalms 31:1, 4-5, 8, 19-21, 23-24 "In You, O Lord I do put my trust (life). I know You will never let me down; for You deliver me in Your righteousness. 4) You pull me out of the net the enemy has laid for me for You are my strength. 5) Into Your hands do I commit my spirit (my soul and my life for You are trustworthy). 8) You have not given me over into the hands of my enemy. You have set my feet in a large place. 19) How great is Your goodness which You have laid up in store for those who love and revere You. It is the goodness You have made for those who trust in You. 20) You hide and protect me in the secret place of Your Presence. You keep me from strife-filled tongues. 21) Blessed are You Lord; for You have shown me Your marvelous loving kindness. 23) Love the Lord, saints; for He preserves the faithful. He plentifully rewards the doer of good. 24) Be of good courage and He shall strengthen the heart of all who hope/trust in Him."

Stage 2: Pupa (he goes into a state of seclusion) **Rewrite the Scripture in your own handwriting.** Then meditate a few minutes on the meaning of these wonderful scriptures. This is important to help get the Word into your heart.

Stage 3: Butterfly (Maturity comes about as you let the Word work in you.) **Read, pray, or sing these verses out loud to God two or three times.** Is your heart grieving? Verse 24 says He will strengthen the heart of all who will put their hope in Him! Let this be your focus today: take the Scripture that speaks the most to you today and speak it all day long.

Journal notes:

DAY 29

Stage 1: Caterpillar (remember he devours much food in preparation) First, read the Scripture to yourself.

Psalms 32: 1-2, 5-11 "Blessed is the man, whose sin is forgiven; whose sin is covered, forgotten by God. 2) Blessed is the man unto whom the Lord does not impute iniquity to him; and in whose spirit there is no guile(deceitfulness). 5) I acknowledged (confessed) my sin unto You Lord. I did not hide my iniquity. I said I will confess my sins unto the Lord; and You forgave all my iniquity. 6) For this reason shall everyone who is godly pray unto You in the time when You may be found. Surely in the floods of great waters they shall not come nigh unto me. 7) **Lord, You are my hiding place.** You preserve me from trouble. You surround me with songs of deliverance. 8) You said You will instruct me and teach me in the way which I shall go. You will guide me with Your eye. 9) Do not be thick-headed. 10) Many sorrows will come to the wicked. But he who trusts in the Lord, mercy shall surround him. 11) Be glad and rejoice in the Lord. Shout for joy, upright in heart."

Stage 2: Pupa (he goes into a state of seclusion) **Rewrite the Scripture in your own handwriting.** Then meditate a few minutes on the meaning of these wonderful scriptures. This is important to help get the Word into your heart.

Stage 3: Butterfly (Maturity comes about as you let the Word work in you.) **Read, pray, or sing these verses out loud to God two or three times.** It is very simple to enter into the mercy promised in verse 10. As we place our trust in God and then shout for joy, we enter into the secret place of God's protection! As you trust God, He surrounds you. Take that thought with you today!

Journal notes:

DAY 30

Stage 1: Caterpillar (remember he devours much food in preparation) First, read the Scripture to yourself.

Psalms 33 "I rejoice in You Lord. Praise is comely for the upright. 2) I praise the Lord with instruments. 3) I sing unto You with a new song. 4) For Your Word is right. All Your Works are truth. 5) You love righteousness and justice (things to be made right). The earth is full of Your Goodness. 6) By Your Word the heavens were made. All the hosts were made by the very breath of Your mouth. 7) You gathered the waters of the sea together as a heap. You lay up the depth in abundance. 8) Let all the earth revere You Lord. Let all the inhabitants stand in awe of You God! 9) For You spoke and it was. You commanded and it stood fast. 10) You bring the plans of the wicked to nothing. You make their devices of no effect (against Your righteous people). 11) It is Your Word Lord that stands forever. The thoughts of Your Heart are to all generations. 12) Blessed is the nation whose God is the Lord! Blessed are the people whom He has chosen for His own inheritance! (That's you and I!) 13) Lord You look from heaven and You behold and see all the sons of men. 14) From Your habitation You see all inhabitants of the earth. 15) You fashioned all hearts alike. You consider all their works. 16) No one is saved by their own strength. 17) Don't rely on horses for safety. They haven't that much strength. 18) But <u>the Lord watches over all who love and revere Him to protect all who will put their hope in His mercy. 19) He will deliver your soul from death. He will keep you alive in times of famine (while the rest of the world is starving).</u> 20) Therefore my soul waits on, trusts in the Lord; for You Lord are my help and my shield. 21) My heart shall rejoice in God because I have trusted in His Holy Name. 23) Let Your mercy Lord be upon us according as we place our hope in You!"

Stage 2: Pupa (he goes into a state of seclusion) **Rewrite the Scripture in your own handwriting.** Then meditate a few minutes on the meaning of these wonderful scriptures. This is important to help get the Word into your heart.

Stage 3: Butterfly (Maturity comes about as you <u>let the Word work in you.</u>)
Read, pray, or sing these verses out loud two or three times to God. Let
this be your focus today: take the Scripture that speaks the most to you today
and speak it all day long.

Journal notes:

DAY 31

Stage 1: Caterpillar (remember he devours much food in preparation) First, read the Scripture to yourself.

Psalms 34: 1-19, 22 "I will bless/praise the Lord at all times. <u>Your Praise shall continually be in my mouth</u> (on my lips). 2) My soul shall boast in You Lord. The humble shall hear and be glad. 3) O magnify the Lord with me. Let us exalt His Name together. 4) I sought the Lord and He heard me and delivered me from all my fears. 5) I look unto You and am enlightened. 6) I cry and the Lord hears and saves me out of all my troubles. <u>7) The angel of the Lord is encamped around about me and my family; and delivers me for I revere God.</u> 8) Oh taste and see that the Lord is good! Blessed is the man that puts his trust in Him. 9) Fear the Lord, ye His saints; for there is no lack (of provision) to those that revere God. 10) The young lions do lack and suffer hunger (at times); but they who seek the Lord shall not want for any good thing. 11) Come ye children, hear me. I will teach you the fear (reverence) of the Lord. 12) What man is there that desires a good and long life? 13) Then he must keep his tongue from evil and from guile (gossip, slander and deceit). 14) Depart from evil and do good. Seek peace and pursue it. (Then you will see a good life, and many days). 15) The eyes of the Lord are upon the righteous. His ears are open to our cry. 16) His face is against those who do evil - to cut them off from the earth. 17) The righteous cry and the Lord hears. He delivers us from all our troubles. 18) The Lord is near those who are of a broken (humbled) heart, and a contrite (repentant) spirit. 19) Many are the afflictions of the righteous. <u>But the Lord</u> delivers us out of them all! 22) The Lord redeems the soul of His servants. None who trust in Him shall be left desolate!" Praise God!

Stage 2: Pupa (he goes into a state of seclusion) **Rewrite the Scripture in your own handwriting.** Then meditate a few minutes on the meaning of these wonderful scriptures. This is important to help get the Word into your heart.

◦◦◦ 🦋 ◦◦◦

Stage 3: Butterfly (Maturity comes about as you <u>let the Word work in you.</u>) **Read, pray, or sing these verses out loud two or three times to God.** By now some darkness is probably being lifted off of you. You have probably begun to feel God's love and faithfulness. He will begin giving you hope and vision for your future! God is so good! Today take verse 7 with you and **speak it all day long**.

Journal notes:

DAY 32

<u>Stage 1: Caterpillar</u> (remember he devours much food in preparation) First, read the Scripture to yourself.

Psalms 35: 5, 8-10, 18-19, 26-28 "Let my enemy be as chaff in the wind (blown clean away)! Let the angel of the Lord chase them! 8) Let the very net they have set (for me) trap them! 9) My soul shall be joyful in You Lord! My soul shall rejoice in Your salvation, Lord! 10) All my bones shall say Lord, who is like You? For You deliver the poor and needy from the thief. 18) I will give thanks in the great congregation. I will praise You among the people. 19) Do not let my enemy rejoice over me. 26) Let my enemy be brought to confusion. 27) Let those who favor my righteous cause shout for joy with me and be glad. Let us <u>say continually</u>: Let the Lord be magnified which has pleasure in the prosperity of His servant! 28) My tongue shall speak of Your righteousness and Your Praise all the day long!"

<u>Stage 2: Pupa</u> (he goes into a state of seclusion) **Rewrite the Scripture in your own handwriting.** Then meditate a few minutes on the meaning of these wonderful scriptures. This is important to help get the Word into your heart.

<u>Stage 3: Butterfly</u> (Maturity comes about as you <u>let the Word work in you.</u>) **Read, pray, or sing these verses out loud two or three times to God.** Declaring victory over your enemy is your faith calling on God to move them. And the Word says God pays attention when He hears faith calling! Do not let grumbling be your reputation with God or man. Grumbling causes downfall. There is a reason why verse 27 says: say continually. Say what? Say whatever God says, not the devil. Let this be your focus today: take the Scripture that speaks the most to you today and speak it all day long.

Journal notes:

DAY 33

<u>Stage 1: Caterpillar</u> (remember he devours much food in preparation) First, read the Scripture to yourself.

Psalms 36: 1, 5-10, 12 "The transgression of the wicked is that there is no fear of God within him. 5) But Your mercy O Lord is as high as the heavens. And Your faithfulness as high as the clouds. 6) Your Righteousness is as mighty as the great mountains. Your justice is as the great deep sea. O Lord, You preserve man and beast alive. 7) How excellent is Your loving kindness, O God. <u>Therefore</u> I put my trust under the shadow of Your wings! 8) And I shall be abundantly satisfied with the blessings of Your house. You shall make me to drink from the river of Your blessings forevermore. 9) For in You is the fountain of life. 10) O Lord, continue Your loving kindness to us as we know You. Continue giving Your Righteousness to the upright in heart 12) (while) the workers of iniquity fall and shall never rise again!"

<u>Stage 2: Pupa</u> (he goes into a state of seclusion) **Rewrite the Scripture in your own handwriting.** Then meditate a few minutes on the meaning of these wonderful scriptures. This is important to help get the Word into your heart.

<u>Stage 3: Butterfly</u> (Maturity comes about as you <u>let the Word work in you.</u>) **Read, pray, or sing these verses out loud two or three times to God.** The beginning of sinning is lacking reverence for God within your heart. Many scriptures talk about the fear (reverence) of God being the beginning of wisdom. To revere God is the foundation of all things that are holy. It is the foundation you must build first in teaching a child. It does not just mean to be awe-struck with God. It does mean a foundation of respect must be built first. This includes love, honor and obeying God. These verses talk about the incredible love, faithfulness, mercy and justice of God. Because of who He is, we can trust Him. Meditate on that today by taking one scripture with you today.

Journal notes:

DAY 34

<u>Stage 1: Caterpillar</u> (remember he devours much food in preparation) First, read the Scripture to yourself.

Psalms 37: 1-9, 11, 14-15 "I shall not fret myself because evil doers appear to be prospering. 2) They shall soon be cut down as the grass is. 3) But I shall trust in You Lord and do good. So shall I dwell in the land and truthfully I shall be fed (and taken care of). 4) I put all my focus and delight in You Lord; for You provide all the desires of my heart! (I shall not need to chase the desires of my heart. I chase You God. I Love You, and You give me all that I long for and that pleases me.) 5) I commit all I do unto You (allowing You to direct me in every decision and aspect of my life.) **[God, I commit this _____ to You. I want Your wisdom in this matter. I will not make a move without You showing me what to do. Your Word says if I will trust in You, You will bring it to pass!]** 6) God You bring forth my righteousness as the (morning) light. You will bring justice as the noonday sun (bright, clear and illuminating. Everyone will see I am righteous and I will be given justice in my life!) 7) Therefore Lord I rest in You and I wait patiently for You (to bring justice). 8) I will cease from anger (for it avails me nothing). I will forsake wrath and revenge. 9) For I know the evil doers shall be cut off; while those who wait on You Lord for justice shall inherit the earth. 11) The meek/humble who are truly trusting in You Lord shall inherit the earth. And they shall be filled with/ rewarded with peace! 14) The wicked plot and plan to kill the righteous; yet 15) their own sword (plan) will destroy them."

<u>Stage 2: Pupa</u> (he goes into a state of seclusion) **Rewrite the Scripture in your own handwriting.** Then meditate a few minutes on the meaning of these wonderful scriptures. This is important to help get the Word into your heart.

Stage 3: Butterfly (Maturity comes about as you <u>let the Word work in you.</u>)
Read, pray, or sing these verses out loud two or three times to God. As
we trust, focus on and delight in the Lord, there is no reason to worry or seek
revenge. Today fill in the blank of the commitment in brackets. Give that
situation to God and trust Him.

Journal notes:

DAY 35

Stage 1: Caterpillar (remember he devours much food in preparation) First, read the Scripture to yourself.

Psalms 37: 16-17, 19, 22-26 "A little in the house of the righteous brings more peace and virtue than the millions that the wicked may have. 17) He will not have it (millions) for long. 19) The righteous (that's me) will have no needs; for in the days of famine God will provide in abundance. 22) Those blessed by God shall inherit the earth. 23) The righteous man's (my) steps are ordered (directed) by the Lord. The Lord delights in that man's (my) ways. 24) Though I may fall, God will not cast me down; for the Lord upholds the righteous man (me) with his own hand! 25) I have never seen the righteous forsaken, nor his children begging for bread. 26) Because the righteous are always merciful to the less fortunate, his own children will be blessed forever!"

Stage 2: Pupa (he goes into a state of seclusion) **Rewrite the Scripture in your own handwriting.** Then meditate a few minutes on the meaning of these wonderful scriptures. This is important to help get the Word into your heart.

Stage 3: Butterfly (Maturity comes about as you let the Word work in you.) **Read, pray, or sing these verses out loud two or three times to God.** Psalms 37 is one of my favorite Psalms because almost every verse is an awesome promise from God for us to claim as ours! Claim some of these verses today as yours.

Journal notes:

DAY 36

Stage 1: Caterpillar (remember he devours much food in preparation) First, read the Scripture to yourself.

Psalms 37: 27-31, 34, 37, 39-40 "Therefore depart from evil and do good. So shall you dwell in safety forever. 28) The Lord loves justice. He does not forsake His saints. He preserves them forever while the wicked are cut off. 29) The righteous shall inherit the land and dwell in it forever! 30) The righteous' mouth speaks wisdom and his tongue talks justice. 31) God's law is in his heart therefore his steps will not falter. 34) Wait on the Lord. Keep His ways and He will exalt you to inherit the land! 37) The righteous man ends up in peace and prosperity. 39) The salvation of the righteous is from the Lord. The Lord is their strength in times of trouble. 40) The Lord will help and deliver them. He will save them because they trust in Him!"

Stage 2: Pupa (he goes into a state of seclusion) **Rewrite the Scripture in your own handwriting.** Then meditate a few minutes on the meaning of these wonderful scriptures. This is important to help get the Word into your heart.

Stage 3: Butterfly (Maturity comes about as you let the Word work in you.) **Read, pray, or sing these verses out loud two or three times to God.** God has a lot to say about the integrity of our heart in these verses, and the rewards of integrity. As you meditate fully on God's promises here, you will gain confidence in the fact that God upholds the righteous. Let this be your focus today: take the Scripture that speaks the most to you today and speak it all day long.

Journal notes:

DAY 37

<u>Stage 1: Caterpillar</u> (remember he devours much food in preparation) First, read the Scripture to yourself.

Psalms 38: 3-4, 11-12, 15, 18, 21-22 "3) There is no soundness in my flesh because of Your anger; neither is there any rest in my bones because of my sin. 4) My sins are way over my head; as a heavy burden they are too heavy for me. 11) My family and friends have left me. 12) My enemy seeks to destroy my life. 15) In You, O Lord do I place my hope for I know that You will hear me when I call unto You. 18) I confess my sin before You O Lord; and I truly repent of it. 21) I know You will not forsake me, Lord. 22) For You are my salvation."

<u>Stage 2: Pupa</u> (he goes into a state of seclusion) **Rewrite the Scripture in your own handwriting.** Then meditate a few minutes on the meaning of these wonderful scriptures. This is important to help get the Word into your heart.

<u>Stage 3: Butterfly</u> (Maturity comes about as you <u>let the Word work in you.</u>) **Read, pray, or sing these verses out loud two or three times to God.** In the first 14 verses of Psalms 38, David talks of his dilemma, his sickness and his enemies. Then in verse 15, he changes his focus to God, and putting his hope in God for redemption. In verses 16-18, David openly declares his sin which opened the door for his enemy to persecute him. He repents of it fully. So, no matter what predicament we find ourselves in or how we got there; we can call on God to help us. If we have sinned, we must repent. I love the fact that David ends this Psalm by declaring that the Lord is his God! No matter what our sins have been, God still wants to be our God. That alone is something to continually praise God for! Let this be your focus today: **God does give second chances!**

Journal notes:

DAY 38

Stage 1: Caterpillar (remember he devours much food in preparation) First, read the Scripture to yourself.

Psalms 39: 7 "My hope is in You, Lord"

Psalms 40:1-8, 10-14, 16-17 "I waited patiently for the Lord; and He inclined unto me and He heard my cry. 2) He brought me up also out of a horrible pit, out of the miry clay. He set my feet upon a rock and established my goings. 3) He has put a new song in my mouth - praise to my God. Many shall see and fear and trust in the Lord. 4) Blessed is the man that makes the Lord his trust; respecting not the proud, nor those who lie. 5) Many O Lord my God are Your wonderful works which You have done and Your thoughts toward us. They cannot be reckoned (counted). If I were to declare them and speak of them, they are more than can be numbered. 6) You have not desired sacrifice or offering from me. For You have opened my ears and my heart. (I will praise You all my days.) 7) Then I said Lo I come; for in the volume of the book it is written of me. 8) I delight to do Your will O my God. Your law is within my heart. 10) I declare Your faithfulness. I speak of Your loving kindness and Your truth in the congregation (before Your people). 11) Withhold not Your tender mercies from me O Lord. Let Your loving kindness and Your truth continually preserve me. 12) Many evils befall me. 13) But I know You will deliver me O Lord. Make haste to help me. 14) Let my enemies be ashamed that seek to destroy my soul. Let them be driven back. 16) But let those who seek You rejoice and be glad in You. They who love Your salvation shall say continually 'The Lord be magnified.' 17) You are my help and my deliverer!"

Stage 2: Pupa (he goes into a state of seclusion) **Rewrite the Scripture in your own handwriting.** Then meditate a few minutes on the meaning of these wonderful scriptures. This is important to help get the Word into your heart.

Stage 3: Butterfly (Maturity comes about as you <u>let the Word work in you.</u>)
Read, pray, or sing these verses out loud two or three times to God. Let this be your focus today: take the Scripture that speaks the most to you today and speak it all day long.

Journal notes:

DAY 39

<u>Stage 1: Caterpillar</u> (remember he devours much food in preparation) First, read the Scripture to yourself.

Psalms 41:1-4, 6, 10-13 "I am blessed because I consider the poor. The Lord will deliver me in my time of trouble. 2) The Lord will preserve me and keep me alive. I am blessed upon the earth. The Lord will not deliver me into the will and hand of my enemy. 3) The Lord strengthens me and brings me up from my sick bed. 4) I said 'Lord, be merciful unto me and heal my soul; forgive my sin.' 6) My enemies may come against me; 10) but the Lord is merciful unto me and raises me up that I may shut the mouth of my adversary! 11) By this I know that You favor me O Lord, because my enemy does not triumph over me! 12) You uphold me in my integrity and set me before Your Face forever. 13) Blessed is the Lord God of Israel from everlasting to everlasting. Amen!"

<u>Stage 2: Pupa</u> (he goes into a state of seclusion) **Rewrite the Scripture in your own handwriting.** Then meditate a few minutes on the meaning of these wonderful scriptures. This is important to help get the Word into your heart.

<u>Stage 3: Butterfly</u> (Maturity comes about as you <u>let the Word work in you.</u>) **Read, pray, or sing these verses out loud two or three times to God.** Praising God strengthens you. It builds joy in your soul, which then feeds healing to your body. Make this your declaration today: **'I praise Your Name, Lord; for You alone are God! You are my God. You are my covering. Your Glory surrounds me! Your Name is upon my forehead forever. I am marked by You as Yours. Demons flee from Your Mighty Presence which is upon me! You make me to be a beacon in the dark. I am lit up with Your Presence. O God, You are holy and You are on me to change the world for your Glory! You are good. You are the Redeemer!'**

Journal notes:

DAY 40

Stage 1: Caterpillar (remember he devours much food in preparation) First, read the Scripture to yourself.

Psalms 42:1-2, 4-5, 8, 11 "As the deer pants after the water brooks, so does my soul pant after You O God! 2) My soul thirsts to see you, the living God. When shall I appear before You? 4) I went to the house of God with the voice of joy and praise. 5) I asked my soul - why are you down cast, depressed? Soul put your hope in God. I shall yet praise God for His help. 8) The Lord will command His loving kindness in the daytime. And in the night His song shall be with me; and my prayer is unto the God of my life. 11) Why are you down cast oh my soul? Put your hope in God. I shall yet praise You. You are health to my body and You are my God!"

Psalms 43 "Judge me O God and deliver me from the deceitful and the unjust man. 2) For You are the God of my strength. 3) O send out Your light and truth that they may lead me. That they may bring me to Your holy hill and to Your tabernacles. 4) Then I will go to Your altar God; unto God who is my exceeding joy. Upon the harp I will sing praise to You O God, my God. 5) Soul put your hope in God. For I shall yet praise God who is health to my body; He is my God."

Stage 2: Pupa (he goes into a state of seclusion) **Rewrite the Scripture in your own handwriting.** Then meditate a few minutes on the meaning of these wonderful scriptures. This is important to help get the Word into your heart.

Stage 3: Butterfly (Maturity comes about as you let the Word work in you.) **Read, pray, or sing these verses out loud two or three times to God.** In chapter 43 we see we can call on God to deliver us from those who hate us. From verse 3, we declare: 'Lord, give me light to see things and truth to know things; Let light and truth lead me so I will know what is right and what Your will is'. (Let this be your declaration today). Remember we are building joy in your soul through praise.

Journal notes:

DAY 41

<u>Stage 1: Caterpillar</u> (remember he devours much food in preparation) First, read the Scripture to yourself.

Psalms 44:1-8 "We have heard with our ears O God. Our fathers have told us the mighty wonders You have performed in their days. (We have read in Your Word also the mighty acts of deliverance You brought about for: Abraham, Isaac, Noah, Jacob, David, Moses, Joseph and so many others. Your acts of deliverance have been passed down by word of mouth for generations from generation to generation.) 2) We've heard how You drove out the heathen with Your Hand; and planted Your people in the good land. 3) They did not receive the good land because of their own ability, strength, money or wisdom. It is Your Arm and Your Arm alone that brings us into great provision and our blessed land. Your light brought them in and brings us in simply because You favor us! 4) Lord, You are my King. You command deliverance for us and for Israel today! 5) <u>Through Your might, we will push back our enemy.</u> <u>Through Your Name we will tread back those who rise up against us.</u> 6) I will not place my trust in my own ability; for I cannot save myself. 7) But You Lord have saved us from our enemy. 8) In You God we boast all day long and praise Your Name forever. We sing Your Praise forever."

<u>Stage 2: Pupa</u> (he goes into a state of seclusion) **Rewrite the Scripture in your own handwriting.** Then meditate a few minutes on the meaning of these wonderful scriptures. This is important to help get the Word into your heart.

<u>Stage 3: Butterfly</u> (Maturity comes about as you <u>let the Word work in you.</u>) **Read, pray, or sing these verses out loud two or three times to God.** Let this be your focus today: take the Scripture that speaks the most to you today and speak it all day long.

Journal notes:

DAY 42

Stage 1: Caterpillar (remember he devours much food in preparation) First, read the Scripture to yourself.

Psalms 45: 1-4, 6-8 "My heart speaks of good things. My tongue is the pen of a ready writer. 2) Grace is poured onto my lips. God has blessed me forever. 3) God has endued me with glory and majesty. 4) In my majesty I ride in prosperity also because truth, meekness and righteousness are with me. 6) God, the scepter of Your Kingdom is a righteous scepter. (Everything about You God is truth, holiness and righteousness.) 7) You love righteousness; and hate wickedness. God, my God, **You have anointed me with the oil of gladness**, even above my peers. (I know Your Hand and Your anointing are upon my head for I feel it, and I see it in my life. You have placed joy in my heart and gratefulness in my soul forever.) 8) You have dressed me so I am dripping with myrrh, aloes and cassia." (These are the anointing oils. They cause a lovely odor and signify belonging to God. The devil and everyone around you can see when you have been anointed and claimed by God. It is like being claimed by the King and given all the best perfumes to anoint your body with. Righteousness is one of the sweetest odors on us. It is there when we accept Jesus. It makes us 'stand out' in a crowd. We can be quickly identified by the world as belonging to the King of the universe.) Verse 2 shows our words should be gracious. Thus God can bless us. Gracious words are only possible when we allow God to heal all unresolved issues and frustrations of our heart. You will find when you have something bothering you deep inside that you have not given over to God; that you just cannot speak gracious/kind words to anyone. <u>There must be healing in the heart</u>. The heart and the tongue are directly connected. That is one purpose for these 150 days of praise. It is training the heart to be joyful and see all the good God does for you. Today, focus on speaking only words that are gracious. If you find there is something bothering you; root it out and give it to God. Then gracious words will flow more easily.

Stage 2: Pupa (he goes into a state of seclusion) **Rewrite the Scripture in your own handwriting.** Then meditate a few minutes on the meaning of these wonderful scriptures. This is important to help get the Word into your heart.

Stage 3: Butterfly (Maturity comes about as you let the Word work in you.) **Read, pray, or sing these verses out loud two or three times to God.** Remember that praising God strengthens you and builds joy in your soul. Memorize the underlined part of verse 7. Speak it all day long.

Journal notes:

DAY 43

Stage 1: Caterpillar (remember he devours much food in preparation) First, read the Scripture to yourself.

Psalms 45: 9, 11-13, 15-17 "Riches and honor shall be in your house. 11) You shall be sought after by kings. 12) The rich will seek you for you are favored. 13) You are wrapped in garments made of gold. 15) With gladness and rejoicing you shall be brought before kings. 16) Your children will be princesses and princes in all the earth. 17) God will make your name to be remembered for all generations (time). Therefore the people shall honor you and praise God forever."

Stage 2: Pupa (he goes into a state of seclusion) **Rewrite the Scripture in your own handwriting.** Then meditate a few minutes on the meaning of these wonderful scriptures. This is important to help get the Word into your heart.

Stage 3: Butterfly (Maturity comes about as you <u>let the Word work in you.</u>) **Read, pray, or sing these verses out loud two or three times to God.** Sometimes during these 150 days of praise, you may find it very challenging to praise. It will seem as if every grouchy demon in the world is attacking, making you feel grouchy. Repent every time and pick your praise up off the ground and continue forward. Don't lie around feeling sorry for yourself or feeling condemned. Condemnation is not of God; because it makes us feel worthless and feel like giving up. The deeper you get into a lifestyle of praise, the more intimacy you will find with God. In praise, you will find strength. Let this be your focus today: take the Scripture that speaks the most to you today and speak it all day long.

Journal notes:

DAY 44

Stage 1: Caterpillar (remember he devours much food in preparation) First, read the Scripture to yourself.

Psalms 46 "Lord, You are my refuge and strength; You are a very present help in times of trouble. 2) So I will not fear. Even if the whole world crumbles and mountains fall into the sea, I will not fear. 3) Though the waters overtake the land. Though mountains quake and tremble. Still I will not fear. 4) There is a river, the streams thereof, make glad the city of our God. This is the holy place of the tabernacles of the most High God. 5) God is in the midst of her therefore she shall not be moved. God will help her and right early. 6) The wicked rage. The kingdoms (of the wicked) were moved. God spoke and the earth melted. 7) The Lord of hosts is with us. God is our refuge. 8) Come. Behold the works of the Lord; the desolations He has made in all the earth. 9) He makes all wars to cease. 10) So be still and know that I am God! I will be exalted among the heathen. I will be exalted in all the earth. 11) Be assured the Lord of hosts is with us. The God of Jacob is our refuge!"

Stage 2: Pupa (he goes into a state of seclusion) **Rewrite the Scripture in your own handwriting.** Then meditate a few minutes on the meaning of these wonderful scriptures. This is important to help get the Word into your heart.

Stage 3: Butterfly (Maturity comes about as you let the Word work in you.) **Read, pray, or sing these verses out loud two or three times to God.** You know if you look around today you will see many lost people acting like there is no God. But God assures us that He will make it clear to them that they have been fooled and have been foolish, when He said I will be exalted among the heathen and in all the earth. They have no choice. They will come to recognize that there is a God; only one and His Name is Adoni - Jehovah, Yahweh! Recognizing that God is God and placing Him totally on the throne of your life is vital to living the good life, the blessed life. We cannot be as the heathen and wait until judgment day to see the truth about letting God be God in our lives. If we expect His protection; if we are His people, then we cannot behave as the heathen (the lost, the wicked) do. We must let the Lord lead us in all things! Let this be your focus today: take the Scripture that speaks the most to you today and speak it all day long.

Journal notes:

DAY 45

Stage 1: Caterpillar (remember he devours much food in preparation) First, read the Scripture to yourself.

Psalms 47 "O clap your hands all ye people. I shout unto You God with the voice of triumph. 2) For You Lord most High are mighty. You are a great King over all the earth. 3) You shall subdue the heathen under us, and the wicked under our feet! 4) You shall choose our inheritance for us. 5) You are gone up with a shout; the Lord is gone up with the sound of a trumpet. 6) I shall sing praises unto my God. Sing praises. Sing praises unto my King. Sing praises. 7) For God is the King of all the earth. I sing praises with understanding. 8) God reigns over the heathen. You sit upon the throne of Your Holiness. 9) The princes of the people are gathered together; the people of the God of Abraham. For the shields of the earth belong to You God. You are greatly to be exalted." Say out loud: 'I shout unto You God with the voice of triumph for You are a mighty God. You are King over all the earth. You subdue the heathen under me. The wicked are under my feet. (Even if you do not feel this way, shout it out anyway. Declare into the atmosphere that God is God!) I sing praises unto you my God; unto my King. I praise and I exalt You Lord for You are God alone! I praise Your holy Name. You are holy, mighty and fearsome to the wicked. But to me You are love!'

Stage 2: Pupa (he goes into a state of seclusion) **Rewrite the Scripture in your own handwriting.** Then meditate a few minutes on the meaning of these wonderful scriptures. This is important to help get the Word into your heart.

Stage 3: Butterfly (Maturity comes about as you <u>let the Word work in you.</u>) **Read, pray, or sing these verses out loud two or three times to God.** Praise God from your heart all day today.

Journal notes:

DAY 46

Stage 1: Caterpillar (remember he devours much food in preparation) First, read the Scripture to yourself.

Psalms 48:1, 9-11, 14 "Great are You Lord and greatly to be praised in the city of our God; in the mountain of Your Holiness. 9) Lord, we have thought on Your loving kindness in the middle of Your temple. We contemplate daily how good You have been to us. 10) According to Your Name O God, so is Your Praise unto the outer parts of the earth. Lord, Your right hand is full of righteousness. (We do not have to fear that You may be an unrighteous Judge.) 11) Let the mountain in the city of Zion shout and rejoice along with us! Let the daughters of your people be glad because You are a just Judge & our God! 14) God is our God forever. And He will personally guide us until the day of our death and passing!"

Stage 2: Pupa (he goes into a state of seclusion) **Rewrite the Scripture in your own handwriting.** Then meditate a few minutes on the meaning of these wonderful scriptures. This is important to help get the Word into your heart.

Stage 3: Butterfly (Maturity comes about as you let the Word work in you.) **Read, pray, or sing these verses out loud two or three times to God.** Talk about the goodness and faithfulness of God today. Even if someone angers you today, stop and start again with praises to God and thoughts of His loving kindness to you. To defeat bad thoughts which bring bad emotions, you must shut them up; and then replace them with praise to God, and thoughts of His faithfulness. The devil wants you to get so bent out of shape over your problems that you cannot see God is still by your side! Even if you fail and give in to negative thoughts and emotions for a time; when you realize it, repent to God for opening the door. Ask for strength to resist; and open your mouth and begin to praise once again! God is faithful to help you! Remember today you will talk about the goodness and the faithfulness of God!

Journal notes:

DAY 47

Stage 1: Caterpillar (remember he devours much food in preparation) First, read the Scripture to yourself.

Psalms 49:6-8, 10-11, 14-15, 17 "Those who boast of and trust in their wealth, 7) none of them can by any means redeem his brother, nor give God a ransom for him. 8) The redemption of the soul is precious. 10) All men die, the rich and the poor. The rich leave their wealth to others. 11) They imagine that their houses go into eternity with them. This just is not so. 14) Death treats all alike. 15) But God redeems my soul from the power of the grave; for He shall receive me. 17) When the rich die, they carry nothing with them."

Stage 2: Pupa (he goes into a state of seclusion) **Rewrite the Scripture in your own handwriting.** Then meditate a few minutes on the meaning of these wonderful scriptures. This is important to help get the Word into your heart.

Stage 3: Butterfly (Maturity comes about as you <u>let the Word work in you.</u>) **Read, pray, or sing these verses out loud two or three times to God.** Verses 6-7 speak of the man who trusts in his riches, yet he cannot buy his soul out of hell. Verse 15 says "but God will redeem my soul (the righteous man's) from the power of the grave (hell). God accomplished this through Jesus. Now man no longer must go to hell. If he has placed his hope in God alone, then that person will be redeemed by God for all eternity! To be honest, we all have deserved hell. If not for the sacrifice of Jesus on our behalf, we would not stand a chance. Money is thought to be the most powerful object on earth. Yet all of Psalm 49 tells how it does not go into eternity with you. It does not impress God. And you cannot buy back your soul once you have crossed over death's threshold and entered into eternity without trusting God for salvation. This gives us the ultimate thing to praise God for; healing now and the fact that He has given us eternal life! Verse 8 says the redemption of your soul is precious to God. And verse 15 says but <u>God has redeemed my soul from the</u> <u>power of the grave (because my trust is in His Son Jesus)</u>! Meditate on that <u>fact today by saying it out loud all day long.</u>

Journal notes:

DAY 48

Stage 1: Caterpillar (remember he devours much food in preparation) First, read the Scripture to yourself.

Psalms 50:1-7 "God, You are a mighty God. You spoke and called all that exists from the rising to the setting of the sun. 2) Out of Zion, the perfection of beauty, God has shined. 3) Our God shall come and shall not keep silence. A fire will go before Him devouring (destroying evil). Everything around Him shall shake and fall apart. 4) He shall call to the heavens from above and to the earth and He shall judge His people. 5) He says: 'Gather My saints together unto me, those who have made a covenant with Me. 6) And the heavens shall declare His righteousness, for God Himself is the Judge. (Think about that!) 7) God says 'Hear Me now. I am God, your God.'"

Stage 2: Pupa (he goes into a state of seclusion) **Rewrite the Scripture in your own handwriting.** Then meditate a few minutes on the meaning of these wonderful scriptures. This is important to help get the Word into your heart.

Stage 3: Butterfly (Maturity comes about as you <u>let the Word work in you.</u>) **Read, pray, or sing these verses out loud two or three times to God.** Whew! How awesome is our God! He just speaks and everything is created from sunrise to sundown. That includes everything in between. We have only to look at creation and marvel at the majesty, the beauty and the wonder of our God. And yet with all His Power, He is good. He desires us to love Him; and to come close so He can pour out His blessings upon us! Covenant is what God is all about. When you covenant with Him as far as He is concerned it is forever. He latches onto you and will not let you go! You declare it. All day today say, 'You are God, <u>my</u> God. And I am in covenant with You!'

Journal notes:

DAY 49

Stage 1: Caterpillar (remember he devours much food in preparation) First, read the Scripture to yourself.

Psalms 50:9-10, 12, 14-17, 19, 21, 23 "God says: 'I am not interested in your bulls, cows and birds that you sacrifice unto Me. 10) If that were all I wanted, all the animals belong to Me and I would just go and take one. The cattle on a thousand hills are Mine. 12) The sacrifice is not for Me to eat. I wouldn't ask you for food. All of the world and everything in it is Mine. 14) <u>Offer unto Me thanksgiving</u> and pay your vows to the Most High God! 15) Then <u>call upon Me in the day of your trouble; and I will deliver you.</u> Your life will bring glory to Me. Through your life and victories I will show the world how faithful I am!' 16) But to the wicked God says, 'You are not in covenant with Me. 17) You have refused Me and My instructions. 19) You have been evil through and through. 21) And you think because there has not been instant judgment that I will let it pass. But I am a righteous God. 23) <u>Remember this: whoever offers praise to Me glorifies Me; and when My covenant people speak blessings, then I will show them My salvation!'</u>"

Stage 2: Pupa (he goes into a state of seclusion) **Rewrite the Scripture in your own handwriting.** Then meditate a few minutes on the meaning of these wonderful scriptures. This is important to help get the Word into your heart.

Stage 3: Butterfly (Maturity comes about as you <u>let the Word work in you.</u>) **Read, pray, or sing these verses out loud two or three times to God.** Write down verses 14, 15 and 23 on a piece of paper. Take them with you today and speak them all day long.

Journal notes:

DAY 50

<u>Stage 1: Caterpillar</u> (remember he devours much food in preparation) First, read the Scripture to yourself.

Psalms 51:1-3 "Have mercy on me O God, according to Your loving kindness. According to the multitude of Your tender mercies, Lord, blot out my sins. 2) Wash me thoroughly from my iniquity and cleanse me from my sin. 3) I acknowledge my sin. It is right in front of my eyes."

<u>Stage 2: Pupa</u> (he goes into a state of seclusion) **Rewrite the Scripture in your own handwriting.** Then meditate a few minutes on the meaning of these wonderful scriptures. This is important to help get the Word into your heart.

<u>Stage 3: Butterfly</u> (Maturity comes about as you <u>let the Word work in you.</u>) **Read these verses out loud to God.** Right away in verse 1 we see the writer David throwing himself on the mercies of God. David is admitting he sinned. He is humbling himself; opening himself up entirely to God and relying on God's mercy and loving kindness; not on his own righteousness. God consistently shows us that a repentant heart is required on our part. The fact that David called on God's mercy (which he said was in great multitude); and on God's loving kindness, shows that **<u>David knew the heart of God is to have mercy and show loving kindness to us.</u>** Our heart must be open for God to do so. In verse 2, David wanted the issue that caused him to sin to be completely dealt with. He did not hold back (reserve) anything in his heart from God's cleansing power. 'Confession is good for the soul' is a saying that has been around a long time. And it is true. But the first confession of our sin should be before the Lord. You might say why confess if He already knows it? It is because confession is the beginning of our repentance of our sin. Confession to God opens our heart to Him. God does not pry our hearts open. We must give Him access. We must face our sin squarely and say yes, I did that and I am sorry. Forgive me God and help me make it right and not go that path ever again. Facing our sin does not mean we have lost our value. Many people cannot face themselves because someone taught them that their sin made them less valuable. God's love for you did not stop just because

you sinned. You certainly wouldn't throw your child away just because they sinned. You would love them anyway. The same goes for God and you. Facing your sin will bring the relief you seek from the pain caused by the sin. And isn't relief from the pain what we all want? Once you confess it to God and open your heart, then He is free to come in and heal you and anyone you may have hurt. Just say, Holy Spirit, come in and heal me in this area. The same principle applies if someone hurt you. Acknowledge your hurt to God. Open your heart and allow Him access to the pain; for God is your healer today. Today openness before the Lord is our focus.

Journal notes:

DAY 51

<u>Stage 1: Caterpillar</u> (remember he devours much food in preparation) First, read the Scripture to yourself.

Psalms 51:7-10, 12, 14-17 "Purge me with hyssop and I shall be clean. Wash me and I shall be whiter than snow! 8) Lord, cause me to hear joy and gladness. Cause me to hope again! 9) Blot out (forever) my iniquities. (That means wash my sins away forever so they cannot be counted against me again!) 10) Create in me a clean heart, O God. Renew a right attitude in me. 12) Restore unto me the joy of Your Salvation! 14) My tongue shall sing aloud of Your Righteousness! 15) My mouth shall speak forth Your Praises! 16) For You God are not interested in the sacrifices I place on the altar. 17) The sacrifices You desire are a broken and a contrite (repentant) heart."

<u>Stage 2: Pupa</u> (he goes into a state of seclusion) **Rewrite the Scripture in your own handwriting.** Then meditate a few minutes on the meaning of these wonderful scriptures. This is important to help get the Word into your heart.

<u>Stage 3: Butterfly</u> (Maturity comes about as you <u>let the Word work in you.</u>) **Read, pray, or sing these verses out loud two or three times to God.** (Verse 7) When You, God, cleanse my heart and pull out all the junk inside, then I feel good. Life feels good again. Maybe you've had pain so long you can't remember ever having hope and joy. God did not design you to live that way. He wants you to have joy and a heart that can hope! Verses 14-15 show it is vital that we praise God for who He is all day long every day. <u>This attitude of reverence, praise and worship will supply us with joy for living a good life.</u> Our bodies will begin to heal because our faith will rise up. Hope will spring forth and life will become good again! Verses 16-17 show us that what God does care about is if I have a humble and repentant heart; a heart that has left off having pride, anger, unforgiveness and arrogance. What pleases God is a heart that is completely open to Him; not resisting His working in it. It's pretty hard to be unforgiving with others when our own sins are staring us in the face. A humbled heart knows it is very capable of sin. It also knows it has been forgiven because of the Grace of God. Therefore we have no right to hold someone else's sin continually against them when we have been forgiven so much by God. Praise God today because you have been forgiven! Today meditate on praise to God and let Him clean out all the junk in your heart.

Journal notes:

DAY 52

Stage 1: Caterpillar (remember he devours much food in preparation) First, read the Scripture to yourself.

Psalms 52: 1, 3, 5-9 "Why do the evil boast in their mischief? Do they not know that the goodness of God is continual? 3) They love evil more than good. Their tongue prefers lying to speaking righteousness. 5) God will remove evil doers from the land of the living. 6) The righteous will see it and know God is God. 7) For the wicked man did not rely on God as his strength; but instead he trusted in the abundance of his riches, which will fail him. 8) **I am like a green (lush, living) olive tree in the house (presence, protection and provision) of (my) God. And I will trust in the mercy of God forever and ever.** (For God is a God of great abundant mercy!) 9) God, I will praise You forever. I will wait on Your Name for it is good before Your saints (people)."

Stage 2: Pupa (he goes into a state of seclusion) **Rewrite the Scripture in your own handwriting.** Then meditate a few minutes on the meaning of these wonderful scriptures. This is important to help get the Word into your heart.

Stage 3: Butterfly (Maturity comes about as you let the Word work in you.) **Read, pray, or sing these verses out loud two or three times to God.** Today memorize verse 8 and speak it out all day long.

Journal notes:

DAY 53

Stage 1: Caterpillar (remember he devours much food in preparation) First, read the Scripture to yourself.

Psalms 53:5 "God will scatter the bones of he (my enemy) who comes against me."

Psalms 54:6-7 "Father, I will praise Your Name O Lord; for it is good. 7) For You have delivered me out of all of my troubles."

Psalms 55:16-18, 22 "As for me, I will call upon God, and the Lord shall save me. 17) Evening, morning and noon I will pray and cry out to You God; and You hear my voice. 18) You deliver my soul in peace from the battle that is against me. 22) I cast my burden upon You Lord, and You sustain me. You will never permit the righteous to be moved (removed)."

Stage 2: Pupa (he goes into a state of seclusion) **Rewrite the Scripture in your own handwriting.** Then meditate a few minutes on the meaning of these wonderful scriptures. This is important to help get the Word into your heart.

Stage 3: Butterfly (Maturity comes about as you <u>let the Word work in you.</u>) Read these verses out loud two times. Then the 3rd time, say I thank You God that...before each sentence. For example on 53:5 say out loud 'I thank You God that You have scattered the bones of my enemy who come against me.' On 54:6-7 say 'I will praise Your Name God for it is good. I thank You God that You have delivered me from all of my troubles.' Go through the rest thanking God for deliverance and His faithfulness to you. **<u>Every time that a grief or problem comes to your mind today just say out loud 'I thank You, Lord, that this is in Your Hands.'</u>** Then begin reciting one of the scriptures above and stir your faith up. Practice now by thanking Him out loud for everything He has done and will do. Spend about 10 minutes thanking God out loud for everything you can think

of. Remember verse 17 assures us that <u>when we cry out, He hears us!</u> Your faith, your trust in God will begin arising with each passing day of these 150 days of praise!

Journal notes:

DAY 54

Stage 1: Caterpillar (remember he devours much food in preparation) First, read the Scripture to yourself.

Psalms 56:1-7 "Thank You God for You are merciful unto me. My enemy tries to overtake me. By fighting daily he tries to oppress me. 2) Daily they come against me and try to swallow me up. There are many who fight against me. <u>But</u> I call on You O Most High God! 3) What time (whenever) I am afraid, I will turn and trust in You. (When fear comes, I will answer by placing my trust in You.) 4) God I will praise You for Your Word. In You God I have placed my trust. I will not (do not; need not) fear what man can do to me. 5) Though every day they come against my words. Their every thought is evil against me. 6) They gather together and set traps for me. They watch my every step and wait for a chance to trap me. 7) Yet they shall not get away with their sins. In Your anger O Lord, You cast down my enemy!"

Stage 2: Pupa (he goes into a state of seclusion) **Rewrite the Scripture in your own handwriting.** Then meditate a few minutes on the meaning of these wonderful scriptures. This is important to help get the Word into your heart.

Stage 3: Butterfly (Maturity comes about as you <u>let the Word work in you.</u>) **Read, pray, or sing these verses out loud two or three times to God.** I find the more I focus on praising God, the less my mind becomes consumed with fear and worry. Peace then moves in. Fear actually diminishes. Fear will become our god when it is what consumes our mind and heart. Whatever we meditate on the most becomes the most powerful thing in our life. So praising God throughout the day elevates God in our mind and heart; and faith arises! That is how we give Him access. That is saying to Him, 'I believe in You. I believe You are bigger than all my problems.' If we focus on our problems all day, we are saying that our problem is bigger than our God. Let this be your focus today: take the Scripture that speaks the most to you today and speak it all day long.

Journal notes:

DAY 55

<u>Stage 1: Caterpillar</u> (remember he devours much food in preparation) First, read the Scripture to yourself.

Psalms 56:8-13 "God, You know everywhere I've been. You have kept every tear (I've cried of a broken heart) in a bottle. You have kept a record of all the wrong done to me (because You care and You will recompense). 9) When I cry out to You, my enemies will turn and run! **<u>This one thing I know: that God is for me!</u>** 10) Therefore I praise You God for Your Word. I praise You Lord for Your Word. 11) I have placed my trust in You. And I will not fear what man can do to me. 12) Your promises are upon my head, O Lord; and in my heart! So I will render praises to You (for that). 13) For You have delivered my soul from death and destruction. You deliver my feet from falling that I may walk before You in the light of the living!"

<u>Stage 2: Pupa</u> (he goes into a state of seclusion) **Rewrite the Scripture in your own handwriting.** Then meditate a few minutes on the meaning of these wonderful scriptures. This is important to help get the Word into your heart.

<u>Stage 3: Butterfly</u> (Maturity comes about as you <u>let the Word work in you.</u>) **Read, pray, or sing these verses out loud two or three times to God.** It amazes me how many times in the scriptures God tells us that He wants to deliver us from our enemies! For God to do that, we must learn to place our lives, situations and our children in His Hands. We must trust Him. The New Testament calls it having faith in God. These 150 days of praise helps us do just that! It focuses on the goodness and marvelous might of our Mighty God so that our faith will arise. As faith in God rises up within us, fear diminishes and we place the situation that bothered us into His Hands. <u>Then things change.</u> He cannot handle it if we are trying to do it ourselves. Only one set of hands can work on an item at one time. Either we will handle it or we will give it to God to handle. But we can't have it both ways. That is not trusting God! Let this be your focus today: take the Scripture that speaks the most to you today and speak it all day long.

Journal notes:

DAY 56

<u>Stage 1: Caterpillar</u> (remember he devours much food in preparation) First, read the Scripture to yourself.

Psalms 57 "Be merciful unto me O God; be merciful unto me; for my soul trusts in You. In the shadow of Your wings I will make my refuge until these calamities pass. (Don't run from God in hard times. <u>Run to Him</u>. Allow His Love to be a covering for you. Seek His defense; don't try to defend yourself.) 2) I will cry unto God Most High; unto God who performs all for me. 3) You send from heaven and save me from my enemy who tries to overtake me. You send forth Your mercy and truth. 4) My soul is among wicked men who want my destruction. 5) Be exalted O God above all the heavens. **<u>Let Your Glory be over all the earth.</u>** 6) Though my enemy sets a trap for me, and hopes I will fall into it; yet it is they who will fall into the trap themselves! 7) My heart is fixed. O God, my heart is fixed on You. I will sing and give praises forever. 8) Awake, my glory awake. I will awake early. 9) And I will praise You. O Lord, I will sing unto You among the heathen (the lost). 10) For Your mercy is so great it is as high as the heavens. (That's a lot of mercy!) Your truth is as high as the clouds in the sky. 11) Be exalted O God above the heavens. Let Your Glory be over all the earth (<u>cover the earth with Your Glory</u>)!"

<u>Stage 2: Pupa</u> (he goes into a state of seclusion) **Rewrite the Scripture in your own handwriting.** Then meditate a few minutes on the meaning of these wonderful scriptures. This is important to help get the Word into your heart.

<u>Stage 3: Butterfly</u> (Maturity comes about as you <u>let the Word work in you.</u>) Say these scriptures out loud at least 2 times, even more if you have time. There is power in your voice as you call out praises unto the Most High God! It is a calling that invites Him. He hears when you cry out in need. And He hears when you invite Him by praising. Praise brings more power on the scene

and in your life than anything else. Praise is like a trumpet sound that says Welcome. Find one scripture here to sing all day long. For me it would be: cover the earth with Your Glory!

Journal notes:

DAY 57

Stage 1: Caterpillar (remember he devours much food in preparation) First, read the Scripture to yourself.

Psalms 58:6-11: "Break the teeth of the wicked (break their power to hurt) O God. 7) Let the wicked melt away the way waters run off; 8) the way a snail melts. 9) Before you know it, God will take the wicked away like a whirlwind. 10) The righteous will see the demise of the wicked and rejoice. (So what do you fear oh man?) 11) For God is a righteous judge in the earth and there is a reward for the righteous!"

Psalms 59:1, 3, 8-9, 16-17: "O God deliver me from my enemies. Defend me from those who rise up against me. 3) They gather against me (unjustly), but I am innocent in this matter. 8) You, Lord, shall have the wicked in derision; for You know their efforts are futile against You. 9) Because of Your strength I will wait (and depend) on You. God, You are my defense! 16) I will sing of Your Power and Might. I will sing aloud of Your Mercy on me in the morning! For You are faithful to be my defense and my place of refuge (where I hide) in my day of trouble. 17) Unto You, O my strength I will sing. For You God are my defense and You God are mercy to me!"

Stage 2: Pupa (he goes into a state of seclusion) **Rewrite the Scripture in your own handwriting.** Then meditate a few minutes on the meaning of these wonderful scriptures. This is important to help get the Word into your heart.

Stage 3: Butterfly (Maturity comes about as you <u>let the Word work in you.</u>) **Read, pray, or sing these verses out loud two or three times to God.** All of Psalm 58 tells us there is justice with God. The wicked will be judged. Every time we read of the psalmists' trouble, we also see where God defended him and totally removed his enemy! In Psalm 59:3, the psalmist said he is innocent in this matter. That was not the requirement which determined whether or not God would defend him. The criterion was the fact that he was a worshipper of the One true God. The wicked were not. That is why the psalmist called God a God of mercy. The fact that you belong to God

is the main thing required for you to call on God's mercy for help. The fact that the psalmist's hands were innocent in the matter helped his cause in the sense that he did not have to be corrected by God. Innocent or guilty, we can throw ourselves on the mercy of God as the psalmist did. His relationship with God was the basis of God hearing his prayer for defense. God is our defender simply because we are His children when we are born again. Your child does not have to be sinless for you to defend them if they are attacked by someone. First you as a parent would stop the attack. So does God. Then you determine if your child was guilty also. If they were guilty also then they would be corrected; they would not be punished but corrected. Punishment does not help correct a child's behavior. <u>Punishment is reserved for the one who refuses to be corrected in love.</u> That is God's way of handling matters. He does not punish you for your sins. Punishment for sin was dealt with on the cross. If you think you are being punished for your sins, the devil is lying to you. Confess sin to God; then remind Satan that it was taken care of on the cross. Correction puts you back on the right path. That is what God is concerned about. God wants to help you. Give Him access by placing your enemy in His Hands. **Sing Psalm 59:16 all day today.**

Journal notes:

DAY 58

<u>Stage 1: Caterpillar</u> (remember he devours much food in preparation) First, read the Scripture to yourself.

Psalms 61 "I know You hear my cry O God; and You attend to my prayer. 2) From the ends of the earth I will cry out to you when my heart is overwhelmed. Lead me to the rock that is higher than I. 3) For You are a shelter to me and a strong tower from the enemy. (You are a covering for me from my enemy!) 4) So I will abide (stay) in Your tabernacle (house) forever. I will trust in the covering of Your wings. 5) For You God have heard my words. You have given me the inheritance of those who reverence Your Name. 6) You will prolong my life (and make it a good, blessed life). 7) I will abide before You/ with You forever. Your mercy and truth shall preserve, keep and protect me. 8) So I will sing unto Your Name forever and I will keep my word to you.

Psalms 62:1-2, 4-8, 10-12: "1) Truly my soul waits for You God. From You alone comes my salvation. 2) You alone are my rock and my salvation. You are my defense. I shall not be greatly moved. 4) Though my enemy is everywhere and full of deceit, 5) my soul relies only on You God. My expectation (for help) is from You. 6) You are my rock and my salvation. Because You are my defense, I shall not be moved. 7) My salvation and my glory is In You God. God, You are the rock of my strength and You are my refuge. 8) I will trust in You at all times. I will pour out my heart to you God. 10) Though riches increase, I will not set my trust in them. 11) God has spoken once; even twice I have heard this: the Power belongs to God. 12) And mercy is of the Lord. You reward every man according to his doings."

<u>Stage 2: Pupa</u> (he goes into a state of seclusion) **Rewrite the Scripture in your own handwriting.** Then meditate a few minutes on the meaning of these wonderful scriptures. This is important to help get the Word into your heart.

<u>Stage 3: Butterfly</u> (Maturity comes about as you <u>let the Word work in you.</u>) **Read, pray, or sing these verses out loud two or three times to God.** We have an enemy that hates us. He is out to take our lives. These are the facts

of life. But the good news is he is not the greatest power in the universe. Our God is. Psalm 61 and 62 continually show us that God will be our defense, our protection. He will be mercy to us. Psalm 61:1 shows our part is to look to Him for help, not anywhere else. Psalm 61:4 shows we must choose to stay in God's protective custody. These are choices we make. That's our part. And God who is truth and mercy will do His part. Declaring these scriptures out loud causes faith to rise up. Faith is like a loud bell to God. The person who believes God can and will do for them is actually giving God access to their life to work miracles. **Find somewhere today to shout out loud that God is your defense, your place of refuge, your covering, and mercy to you! Let faith arise and God will scatter your enemies!**

Journal notes:

DAY 59

Stage 1: Caterpillar (remember he devours much food in preparation) First, read the Scripture to yourself.

Psalms 63 "O God, You are my God. Early will I seek you. My soul, it thirsts for You. My heart is longing for You, in a dry and thirsty land, where no water is. (But I shall rejoice in God!) 2) To see Your Power and Your Glory as I have seen You in Your Sanctuary. (And I shall rejoice in God!) 3) Your loving kindness is better to me than life. My lips shall forever praise You. (And I shall rejoice in God!) 4) Thus will I bless You while I live. I will lift up my hands in Your Holy Name. (So I shall rejoice in God!) 5) My soul shall be satisfied; and my mouth shall praise You. (Thus I shall rejoice in my God!) 6) I will remember You. Even in the night I will think about Your Faithfulness to me. (And I shall rejoice in my God!) 7) You have been my help. In the shadow of Your wings I shall rejoice. (I will rejoice in You God!) 8) My soul truly longs for You God. For Your Right Hand, it holds me up. (I will rejoice in You God!) 9) Those who seek my soul, to destroy; shall go down to the lower parts of the earth. 10) They shall fall by the sword. 11) But I shall rejoice in You God! Every one that swears by You shall glory! And the mouths of my enemies shall be stopped." (I shall rejoice in You Lord. I shall rejoice in my God!)

Stage 2: Pupa (he goes into a state of seclusion) **Rewrite the Scripture in your own handwriting.** Then meditate a few minutes on the meaning of these wonderful scriptures.

Stage 3: Butterfly (Maturity comes about as you <u>let the Word work in you.</u>) This one sing out loud instead of reading it. It doesn't matter if the tune you use is odd, or if your voice is out of tune. Sing from your heart to God's heart. Sing all day: I shall rejoice in You God!

Journal notes:

DAY 60

<u>Stage 1: Caterpillar</u> (remember he devours much food in preparation) First, read the Scripture to yourself.

Psalms 64:10: "The righteous shall be glad in the Lord, and shall trust in Him; for all the upright in heart shall glory." (Whatever is not going well in your life right now, just begin to declare that God is your defense as it says in this verse. Declare out loud: God is still on His throne and worthy to be praised for He will set all things right for me.)

Psalms 65:1-3, 5-13 "I praise You O God for 2) You hear my prayer. Unto You all flesh looks for defense. 3) I praise You God for You purged my sins (on the cross). Blessed is the man whom You have chosen and who calls out to You; for he will dwell with You forever. I shall be satisfied with the goodness of Your house, and Your holy sanctuary. 5) By mighty things, and in righteousness You answer us O God. We are confident in Your salvation. 6) By Your strength You set the mountains in place. 7) By Your Love and Mercy You still/calm the sea and the people. 8) You make the morning and the evening to rejoice! 9) You visit the earth and water it. You greatly enrich it with the river of God. You prepare food and all good things. 10) You water and You bless the springing forth of all growing things. 11) You crown the year with Your goodness; and wherever You are brings abundance (of joy, peace, blessings). 12) Health, beauty and abundance are everywhere You are. The earth and its people rejoice because of Your goodness. 13) The earth shouts for joy and sings at the Presence of our God!"

<u>Stage 2: Pupa</u> (he goes into a state of seclusion) **Rewrite the Scripture in your own handwriting.** Then meditate a few minutes on the meaning of these wonderful scriptures. This is important to help get the Word into your heart.

<u>Stage 3: Butterfly</u> (Maturity comes about as you <u>let the Word work in you.</u>) **Read, pray, or sing these verses out loud two or three times to God.** Declare Psalm 65 over and over. Magnify God with your mouth and His

peace will override all fear and anxiety you may have. Fear is offered to you by the devil. But you must make a choice to remain in the peace of God. Shout praises to God until fear is chased away. **Magnify the Lord; not your problems!**

Journal notes:

DAY 61

<u>Stage 1: Caterpillar</u> (remember he devours much food in preparation) First, read the Scripture to yourself.

Psalms 66 "Make a joyful noise unto God, all ye people and lands. 2) Sing forth the honor of His Name. Make His praise glorious. 3) Say to God -How wondrous and mighty are Your works! Through the greatness of Your Power Your enemies shall submit themselves to You. (Let us never forget there is no one mightier than our God Jehovah!) 4) All the earth shall worship You and shall sing praises unto You. They shall sing of Your Name! 5) Oh come and see the works of our God. You are mighty toward the children of men. 6) You turned the sea into dry land. The people went through on foot. There we did rejoice in You! 7) You rule by Your Power forever! Your eyes behold and see the heathen. (God is not blind to the actions of the wicked.) Let not the rebellious exalt themselves (for they are not more powerful than God is.) 8) O bless our God, people. Make the voice of praise to Him be heard (everywhere). 9) God holds our soul in life! God will not permit our feet to be moved! (He will not allow our enemies to overthrow us as long as we keep Him as our God!) 10) You God have proven us and tried us as silver is tried. 11) You brought us into the net and trials were laid upon us. 12) You allowed men to ride over our heads (to be our superiors). We went through fire and water. (We went through the purification process.) Then You brought us out (on the other side) into our wealthy place! 13) God, I will go to Your house of worship with my sacrifice because I am so thankful to You. I will pay the vows I declared to You, 14) which my mouth spoke and promised when I was in trouble and You came to my rescue! 15) I will give my finest offering. 16) Come and hear all you who revere God and I will declare (tell you) what He has done for my soul! 17) (When I was in trouble and grief), I cried out to Him with my mouth. I praised Him with my tongue. 18) For I knew if I held onto iniquity in my heart and would not repent, the Lord would not hear (give audience to) me in my pleas. 19) But God truly has heard me. He has given attention to the voice of my prayer. (God is living and He hears me!) 20) O blessed is God for He has not turned away my prayer, nor His mercy from me!"

Stage 2: Pupa (he goes into a state of seclusion) **Rewrite the Scripture in your own handwriting.** Then meditate a few minutes on the meaning of these wonderful scriptures. This is important to help get the Word into your heart.

Stage 3: Butterfly (Maturity comes about as you <u>let the Word work in you.</u>) **Read, pray, or sing these verses out loud two or three times to God.** Our singing to Him is more beautiful than even the angels! We are to sing forth praises to God. As we do, joy will begin to bubble up in us. Verse 8 is saying lift up your voice; make praises to God be heard in the land. Praise to God must be heard in this nation! In the Old Testament, God showed us how that when the whole nation of Israel gathered and their voices were raised in praise to Him; His Presence came on the scene in a mighty way; and great deliverance was brought by His mighty Hand! By that He is showing us the need for and the power of group praise! Let praise be heard in this land! The enemy cannot take you out or move you from God's goodness and purpose when you remain/stay in praise (verse 9)! Praisers have joy and victory; while grumblers do not. Silver is put through a system which causes impurities to come to the surface where it is scraped off. When the system is completed - the silver is pure and much, much stronger (vs. 10)! This also applies to you and me! Praise is the order of the day; so let nothing keep you from it!

Journal notes:

DAY 62

Stage 1: Caterpillar (remember he devours much food in preparation) First, read the Scripture to yourself.

Psalms 67 "God be merciful to us, and bless us; God cause Your face and favor to shine upon us. 2) That Your way may be known upon the earth; and Your saving health be among all nations/kingdoms/countries. 3) Oh let the people praise You O God. Let all the people praise You! 4) O let the nations (people in all the earth) be glad and sing for joy; for You shall judge the people in righteousness, and govern the people upon the earth. (You are a righteous judge!) 5) Oh let the people praise You O God. **Let all the people praise You. 6) Then shall the earth yield her increase; and God, our God shall bless us!** 7) God shall bless us and all the ends of the earth shall revere Him (for He is a mighty God)!"

Psalms 68:1-4 "**Let God arise and His (and our) enemies be scattered!** Also let them that hate Him flee before Him! 2) As smoke is, so let our enemy be that is quickly driven away. As wax melts in the heat of fire, so do the wicked perish at the Presence of our God. 3) But the righteous are glad and rejoice before the Lord. The righteous are exceedingly joyful. 4) Sing to God. Sing praises to His Name. Exalt Him, who rides upon the heavens, by His Name JAH. Rejoice before the Lord!"

Stage 2: Pupa (he goes into a state of seclusion) **Rewrite the Scripture in your own handwriting.** Then meditate a few minutes on the meaning of these wonderful scriptures. This is important to help get the Word into your heart.

Stage 3: Butterfly (Maturity comes about as you let the Word work in you.) Speak these scriptures out loud as praises to God. Psalm 67:1-6 shows there is a connection between praising God and the blessing of the Lord upon us. In 67:4, we see that God is a righteous judge. People everywhere are clamoring for justice. Well, there it is. God is a righteous judge. So if we are done wrong, then we need to just tell God - not our friends and relatives how some person has wronged us. Our friends, relatives and co-workers can do nothing about

it. But <u>God is our righteous judge</u>. If we are innocent, He will handle it; that is if we will leave it in His Hands. Two things can prevent us from getting justice: 1) If we continually talk about the injustice; and 2) if we take matters into our own hands, taking it out of God's hands. Today praise God and place your defense in His hands and leave it there!

Journal notes:

DAY 63

Stage 1: Caterpillar (remember he devours much food in preparation) First, read the Scripture to yourself.

Psalms 68:5-13, 17-19, 21, 28, 32-35 "God is a Father to the fatherless and justice for the widows. 6) God gives a family to the lonely! He frees those who are bound by chains (addictions or emotional hurts that hold us in darkness). 7) O God when You went in front of Your people who came out of captivity; when You marched through the wilderness with Your people 8) the earth shook. The heavens dropped at the Presence of our mighty God! Even Mt Sinai shook and was moved at the Presence of God; the God of Israel! 9) You sent plentiful rain. By that provision You confirmed the people were Yours! When they were weary, You sustained them (as You do us when we are weary)! 10) Your people dwell in a place of provision! You O God have prepared of Your goodness for the poor! 11) You gave the word and many spread it abroad. 12) You cause our enemies to flee! We divide the spoil of the enemy among us. 13) Though we have lain among the ashes, yet we will be as the wings of a dove covered in silver and her feathers covered with yellow gold. (Though we were once covered in ashes, we now are covered in beauty!) 17) The chariots of God are twenty thousand and thousands of angels. The Lord is among them as He was in Mt Sinai, in the Holy Place. 18) He has ascended on high. **He has led the captive out of bondage!** 19) Blessed is the Lord who daily loads us with blessings for He is the God of our salvation! 21) God, You wound the head of our enemy and the head of he who refuses to turn from his sins. 28) My God has commanded my strength to be. God has worked it all out for me! 32) Sing to God, ye people of the earth. Sing praises to the Lord. 33) Sing to Him who rides upon the heavens of heavens, for He sends out His mighty voice. 34) Ascribe strength unto God (recognize and praise God for His Power). 35) God, You are mighty in Your Holy place. It is You God who gives strength and might unto Your people. Blessed be our God!"

Stage 2: Pupa (he goes into a state of seclusion) **Rewrite the Scripture in your own handwriting.** Then meditate a few minutes on the meaning of these wonderful scriptures. This is important to help get the Word into your heart.

Stage 3: Butterfly (Maturity comes about as you <u>let the Word work in you.</u>)
Read, pray, or sing these verses out loud two or three times to God.
Verse 6 says clearly <u>God frees those who are bound by (the devil's) chains!</u>
That reveals that it is God's Will for people to be free! Chains represent any
demonic hold that is in our life. God's Power can free us; for greater is God's
Power than the power of the devil. Plus if we are born again; then we have
become God's child, and God wants His children free! I see so many people
bound by chains. Most know it but feel they are trapped without hope. Some
are too angry to allow God to free and heal them. The chains are created by
the devil, not by God. The devil is evil; he intends evil for people. The only
way the devil can maintain control and keep people in addictions, disease,
mental torment and other darkness is for him to trick them into choosing
him or believing him over God. Let this be your focus today: Declare all day
verses 5-6 with this: 'God is my Father. He has freed me from all bondage.'

Journal notes:

DAY 64

Stage 1: Caterpillar (remember he devours much food in preparation) First, read the Scripture to yourself.

Psalms 69: 1-18, 29-36 "Save me, O God, for my circumstances are flooding my soul. 2) I am sinking and everything is over my head. 3) I have cried until I cannot cry any longer. 4) Those who hate me without cause are more than me. It is not fair for I restored what I took not. 5) God, You know all my sins. This is not one of them. 6) Lord, do not let those who wait on You be ashamed. Do not let down those who seek You! 7) It is because I love You that my enemies hate me. 8) Even my own family has turned against me. 9) Love for You has consumed me. I am hated because I love You. 10) I wept and fasted, 11) wore grieving clothes and became a curse word to them. 12) The elders are even speaking against me. 13) But as for me, my prayer is unto You! In the multitude of Your mercy, I know You hear me. Also in the truth of Your salvation, 14) You deliver me out of this mess. You will not let me drown. You will deliver me from those who hate me. 15) You will not let death come to me. 16) I know You hear me, O Lord. For Your loving kindness is good. You turn to me according to the multitude of Your tender mercies! 17) You do not hide Your Face from me. When I am in trouble, You hear me speedily! 18) You draw near to my soul; and redeem it. You deliver me! 29) Let Your salvation O God set me on high (raise me out of this dilemma). 30) I praise the Name of God with a song. I magnify You with thanksgiving. 31) <u>Praise is more pleasing to You than sacrificing an ox at the altar.</u> (You are pleased with my praise!) 32) The humble shall be glad. The heart that seeks God will have life! 33) Lord, You hear the cry of the poor and needy. You do have pity on the ones held captive (by the devil). 34) Let all the heavens and the earth praise You; all the seas and everything in it praise You Lord! 35) For You save Your people and provide a place for them. 36) Their children and their grandchildren shall have an inheritance there. Those who love You shall dwell safely with You forever!"

Stage 2: Pupa (he goes into a state of seclusion) **Rewrite the Scripture in your own handwriting.** Then meditate a few minutes on the meaning of these wonderful scriptures. This is important to help get the Word into your heart.

Stage 3: Butterfly (Maturity comes about as you <u>let the Word work in you.</u>) **Read, pray, or sing these verses out loud two or three times to God.** Notice King David (who wrote this) began by pouring his heart out to God. But he finished by giving praise to God! Once we have poured out our hearts to God; then we must turn to magnifying Him in order for faith to arise and God to be able to work on our behalf. Notice that even though he was innocent in this matter, he remained humble and dependant on God for justice. If we are completely innocent, yet we become arrogant about it and try to get justice ourselves, then we become as guilty as the other party. And God must correct us also. So <u>we need to learn to trust God to defend, to heal and to restore all relationships that should be.</u> Notice also David was hurt by his own family. Those hurts are deeper. But magnify God's goodness as in verses 13-36 and let God heal you and restore all! Let this be your focus today: take the Scripture that speaks the most to you today and speak it all day long.

Journal notes:

DAY 65

Stage 1: Caterpillar (remember he devours much food in preparation) First, read the Scripture to yourself.

Psalms 70:4 "Let all those who seek You rejoice and be glad in You. Let those who love Your salvation say continually 'Let God be magnified.'"

Stage 2: Pupa (he goes into a state of seclusion) **Rewrite the Scripture in your own handwriting.** Then meditate a few minutes on the meaning of these wonderful scriptures. This is important to help get the Word into your heart.

Stage 3: Butterfly (Maturity comes about as you let the Word work in you.) **Read, pray, or sing these verses out loud two or three times to God.** Say continually, over and over: Let God be magnified! As you say this all day today think about what it means. You can add 'Let God be magnified in this situation.' Or 'Let God be magnified in that situation.' What you are doing is putting God (back) on the throne in your heart and in your life! I believe part of exalting God (to His rightful place as King) is humbling ourselves to bow before Him. Sometimes subconsciously we become full of pride over 'our' righteousness. We forget it isn't ours at all. We live fully under the righteousness of Jesus. We did nothing worthy of it. Remembering that is humbling. The robe of righteousness was bought at the price of Jesus' life; and then placed on us. We are not righteous without it! Let God be magnified; for He alone is worthy of our praise. He redeemed/redeems us. He restored/restores us. Let God be magnified!

Journal notes:

DAY 66

<u>Stage 1: Caterpillar</u> (remember he devours much food in preparation) First, read the Scripture to yourself.

Psalms 71 "In You O Lord, do I place my trust. You will never let me be put to confusion. 2) You deliver me in Your righteousness and cause me to escape (the enemy's traps). You lean Your ear to me and hear my requests! 3) You are my strong habitation (place of refuge) for I continually run to You. You have given commandment to save me. You are my rock and my fortress. 4) You deliver me out of the hand of the wicked; out of the hand of the unrighteous and cruel. 5) You are my hope O Lord God; and my trust from the time I was a youth (very young). 6) By You I have been held up from the time I was in my mother's womb. You brought me out. My praise will be continually to You. 7) You are my strong refuge. 8) Let my mouth be filled with praise to You with glory and honor all day long! 9) You will not cast me off in my old age or when my strength is gone. 10) Though my enemies lay wait for my soul, 11) thinking there is no one to deliver me, 12) yet You God are a ready help. You make haste and deliver me from them. 13) May they be confused and swallowed up in shame for they seek to harm me. 14) But I will continually (place my) hope in You. And I will praise You more and more. 15) <u>My mouth will speak of Your righteousness and deliverance all day long!</u> 16) And I will go in Your strength. I will declare (to everyone that) You are righteous and You alone. 17) O God, You have taught me from the time I was very young. And so I will tell the world of your wondrous works! 18) When I am old and gray, You will not forsake me. I will teach the next generation of Your strength. I will talk of Your power to the generation to come. 19) Your Righteousness is very high indeed. Who has done great and mighty things like You? O God, who is like You?! (No one!) 20) You have brought me through many troubles (dilemmas). You have revived me. And You will bring me back from death. 21) You increase me and comfort me on every side. 22) I will praise You with music. I will sing of Your truth O God, O Holy One of Israel. 23) My lips shall greatly rejoice when I sing to You. And my soul will be joyful because You have redeemed me. 24) I will speak of Your Righteousness all day long; for You have confused and shamed my enemy who seek to hurt me."

Stage 2: Pupa (he goes into a state of seclusion) **Rewrite the Scripture in your own handwriting.** Then meditate a few minutes on the meaning of these wonderful scriptures. This is important to help get the Word into your heart.

Stage 3: Butterfly (Maturity comes about as you <u>let the Word work in you.</u>) **Read, pray, or sing these verses out loud two or three times to God.** Let this be your focus today: take the Scripture that speaks the most to you today and speak it all day long.

Journal notes:

DAY 67

Stage 1: Caterpillar (remember he devours much food in preparation) First, read the Scripture to yourself.

Psalms 72:18-19 "Blessed be the Lord God who alone does wondrous (and mighty) works. 19) Blessed be His Glorious Name forever. Let the whole earth be filled with His glory."

Psalms 73:1, 3-9, 11, 13-14, 17-28 "Truly God is good to Israel (His people), to those who are of a clean heart. (A clean heart does not mean we are perfect. It is talking about a heart that truly loves God and allows God to cleanse it daily by His Word.) 3) But I was envious when I saw the prosperity of the wicked. 4) It looked like their strength (power) would never fail. 5) It looked like they did not have grief and suffering as the righteous did. 6) Because all was going well for them, they were full of pride, arrogance and violence against others. (They thought they could not be brought down.) 7) They had more than they needed. 8) They were full of themselves. 9) They arrogantly spoke against God. 11) They really thought no one could bring them down, even God. 13) So I thought, I have been righteous for nothing. 14) I have been through grief and trials. I am continually corrected by God. (This was very upsetting to me.) 17) Until I went to God about this matter. Then He showed me their end! 18) I saw that they were going into eternal destruction, 19) to live in darkness and terror forever. 20) My eyes were opened to the truth and I saw how God despises wickedness. 21) I repented. 22) I said to God; I was such a fool. I was ignorant of the truth. 23) I will continually stay with You, God. For You uphold me with Your right hand. 24) God, You guide me with Your counsel. Afterward, You will receive me into glory (while the wicked are punished forever)! 25) There is nothing more important to me than You God. 26) Though my flesh fails - yet God will strengthen me. 27) Those who hate You will perish forever. (So correct me, God. I welcome it; and I am glad for it. Keep me on the right path; the path of life!) 28) But as for me, it is good for me to draw close to God. I will put my trust in the Lord God. I will then declare (tell others about) all Your Glorious acts to men!" (Our hearts are changed as we ingest the Word of God.

Little by little our children learn to behave better, to read and write. So little by little, God matures us also. It is His very Presence that changes us as we sit in His Presence and just 'soak up' His Glory. Speaking praises out to God is welcoming Him into your heart to change you. As we change, so do our circumstances. Instead of chasing change in our life, we need to chase God and love Him. Then all else will change!)

Stage 2: Pupa (he goes into a state of seclusion) **Rewrite the Scripture in your own handwriting.** Then meditate a few minutes on the meaning of these wonderful scriptures. This is important to help get the Word into your heart.

Stage 3: Butterfly (Maturity comes about as you let the Word work in you.) **Read, pray, or sing these verses out loud two or three times to God.** Let this be your focus today: take the Scripture that speaks the most to you today and speak it all day long.

Journal notes:

DAY 68

Stage 1: Caterpillar (remember he devours much food in preparation) First, read the Scripture to yourself.

Psalms 75:1, 5-10: "Unto You, God we give thanks. We give thanks to You, for Your Name is with us. Your wondrous (mighty) works show it. 5) Lift not up your heart unto pride, oh man. 6) For promotion is neither from the east, west, nor the south. 7) But God is judge. He puts down one and sets up another! 8) And be assured, God brings justice! 9) I will declare forever and sing praises to the God of Jacob! 10) The wicked will be cut off. The righteous shall be exalted!"

Psalms 76:1-9, 12 "In Judah, God is known. His Name is great (holy, respected) in Israel. 2) His Holy tabernacle is in Jerusalem. His dwelling place is in Zion. 3) You, God have broken the tools of war. 4) You are more glorious and excellent than any! 5) You are more powerful than all the wicked men. 6) At Your rebuke the wicked are cast away. 7) You are to be feared by the wicked and revered by the righteous. Who can stand against You? 8) You caused justice to be heard from heaven. The earth feared and was still, 9) when You, God arose to judgment. You arose to save the meek, the humble, and those who are dependant on You! 12) You God are a mighty God!"

Stage 2: Pupa (he goes into a state of seclusion) **Rewrite the Scripture in your own handwriting.** Then meditate a few minutes on the meaning of these wonderful scriptures. This is important to help get the Word into your heart.

Stage 3: Butterfly (Maturity comes about as you <u>let the Word work in you.</u>) **Read, pray, or sing these verses out loud two or three times to God.** Writing every morning and praising out loud reminds and assures us of God's Love for us; and His ability to defend and care for us. Some times I think

we have forgotten just how awesome God is! Let God arise and our enemies be scattered! Let this be your focus today: take the Scripture that speaks the most to you today and speak it all day long.

Journal notes:

DAY 69

Stage 1: Caterpillar (remember he devours much food in preparation) First, read the Scripture to yourself.

Psalms 77:1-3, 10-15, 20 "I cried to God with my voice, and He gave ear (paid attention) to me! 2) In the day of my trouble I sought the Lord. 3) My spirit was overwhelmed. 10) I said, I will remember the blessings of the Most High unto me. 11) I will remember all His mighty acts of the past. 12) <u>I will meditate on all He has done. I will talk continually of the Lord's blessings!</u> 13) Who is greater than our God? 14) You are the God that does mighty wonders (in the earth)! Your strength is declared among the people. 15) With Your Arm, Your people are redeemed. 20) You led Your people like a flock by the hand of Moses and Aaron."

Stage 2: Pupa (he goes into a state of seclusion) **Rewrite the Scripture in your own handwriting.** Then meditate a few minutes on the meaning of these wonderful scriptures. This is important to help get the Word into your heart.

Stage 3: Butterfly (Maturity comes about as you <u>let the Word work in you.</u>) **Read, pray, or sing these verses out loud two or three times to God.** Even when things are not going our way, or well at all; still this Psalm shows us we are to focus our eyes on the blessings which the Lord gives us. We are to remember all He has already done! Verse 12 shows me that Satan will try to get us to think and talk continually about our problems; but we are to meditate on and talk about God's goodness continually instead. Then God can come in and change things. There is a Scripture that says "hope deferred makes the heart sick..." (Proverbs 13:12). What that means is when the human spirit has no hope for anything ever changing - then nothing will change; and life is unbearable. But focusing on the goodness and the faithfulness of God gives us hope and makes it possible for things to change! Focusing on the negatives kills hope and shuts out possibilities of it ever changing. The rest of Proverbs 13:12 says "...but when the desire comes, it is a tree of life." When we get hope again and see God working, we have life again in our soul.

When our soul heals, then our body heals also! ***Focusing on, continually thinking of, and talking about the bad brings death.*** While ***focusing on, continually thinking of, and talking about God's goodness and blessings to us brings health and life!*** Think about it! Let this be your focus today: take the Scripture that speaks the most to you today and speak it all day long.

Journal notes:

DAY 70

Stage 1: Caterpillar (remember he devours much food in preparation) First, read the Scripture to yourself.

Psalms 78: 4-8, 12-15, 22-25, 32 "We will tell our children about the praises of the Lord, His strength and His wonderful works which He has done! 5) For He established a testimony of His goodness by what He did for Jacob. He commanded that the law be taught to the children, 6) that they might know God and His law; 7) so that the children would set their hope in God, never forgetting His mighty works, keeping His commandments; 8) and that the children would not be stubborn-headed nor rebellious toward God as their forefathers were. Teach the children so their heart will be set aright and their spirit steadfast with God. 12) Remember how powerful God's deliverance was to the Israelites (and to you in your time of trouble)! 13) God divided the sea for the Israelites, and caused dry land to appear so that they could walk through and escape their enemy. Never forget that. 14) In the daytime He led them by a cloud and at night by a visible fire in the sky! 15) When they needed water, He caused water to come from a rock and gave water to more than one million people! 22) Yet they turned right around afterward and believed not in God, and trusted not in His salvation. 23) He commanded the clouds from above and opened the doors of heaven! 24) And food rained from heaven. 25) The food of angels was given them. 32) And after all this, they sinned still and believed not though they had seen His mighty, amazing and wondrous works (on their behalf)."

Stage 2: Pupa (he goes into a state of seclusion) **Rewrite the Scripture in your own handwriting.** Then meditate a few minutes on the meaning of these wonderful scriptures. This is important to help get the Word into your heart.

Stage 3: Butterfly (Maturity comes about as you let the Word work in you.) **Read, pray, or sing these verses out loud two or three times to God.** God calls unbelief evil. Unbelief is seeing, yet having a hardened heart and not believing. Seeing God work on our behalf should humble us and break off hardness in us. You may say, what has God ever done for me that I may praise

Him for it? Dear, when we have so much grief and pain, it is hard to praise God. Remember 'hope deferred makes the heart sick'? But **praise brings hope back.** God has done more for you than you will ever be able to recount. 1) You are alive. 2) He sent His innocent Son to be beaten and die because you sinned. Accepting forgiveness is all you have to do to be forgiven. You cannot earn forgiveness from God. It is a free gift to you if you will accept it. That alone is reason for praise. Salvation is the greatest gift available to mankind. It is free. It is already paid for! Just spend some time today being thankful for the priceless gift of salvation. Where would you be without Christ? This is the first step out of a dark depression. Then as things come to mind of other things to be thankful for, write them down and sing to God thanking Him with a sincere heart!

Journal notes:

DAY 71

Stage 1: Caterpillar (remember he devours much food in preparation) First, read the Scripture to yourself.

Psalms 78:32-35, 37-40, 42, 52-55, 65-66, 68-70 Take note as you read how faithful God is even to this ungrateful people. "Because the people turned from God and sinned, and would not believe God although they had seen all His miracles and provision...33) Therefore their days became consumed with misery and their years with trouble. 34) When their troubles started causing deaths, then they sought Him. They returned to Him and sought Him early in the mornings. 35) They remembered that God was their rock; and the high God was their redeemer. 37) Yet their heart still was not totally right with God. Neither were they faithful in keeping covenant with Him. 38) But God, full of compassion, forgave their iniquity. Many times He turned His wrath and did not punish them though they deserved it. 39) He knew they were but flesh. 40) They turned again and tried God's patience; (by doing so) they limited the Holy One. 42) They forgot how He had delivered them from their enemy. 52) God led His own people out like sheep and guided them in the wilderness like a flock. 53) God led them in safety so they did not need to fear; while their enemy was drowned in the sea behind them! 54) He brought them to the border of the land they were to inherit where God would reside with them. 55) He kicked out their enemy for them. (Again they turned away from God; and troubles came upon them because God removed His Hand of protection.) 65) Then in His eternal mercy, 66) God smote their enemy. 68) He chose the tribe of Judah (which means PRAISE). 69) He chose to live among His people again. 70) And He gave them David as a leader for His people!"

Stage 2: Pupa (he goes into a state of seclusion) **Rewrite the Scripture in your own handwriting.** Then meditate a few minutes on the meaning of these wonderful scriptures. This is important to help get the Word into your heart.

Stage 3: Butterfly (Maturity comes about as you <u>let the Word work in you.</u>) **Read, pray, or sing these verses out loud two or three times to God.** Doesn't verses 32-33 sound like our world today? Haven't we also as a whole turned from serving God; and brought calamity upon ourselves? Verse 40 shows we can limit how much God can do in our lives! Verse 42 shows that mankind has a gratitude problem. God showed many, many signs and wonders when He delivered His people out of bondage in Egypt. He clearly showed all nations at that time who He was for when He brought 10 horrible plagues on Egypt and its people. Just how much of God defending us does it take for us to remember He is for us today and He is worthy of our praise? Let this be your focus today: take the Scripture that speaks the most to you today and speak it all day long.

Journal notes:

DAY 72

Stage 1: Caterpillar (remember he devours much food in preparation) First, read the Scripture to yourself.

Psalms 81:1-7, 10, 13-16 "(We) sing out loud unto God (for You are) our strength. (We) make a joyful noise (celebration) unto You, God of Jacob. 2) (We) speak a psalm and play the musical instruments. 3) We keep and celebrate Your appointed feasts. 4) For this was a (required) statute (by You) unto Israel and it was Your law. 5) You ordained feasts and Praise when we left the land of bondage. 6) You removed my shoulder from the burden; and delivered my hands from the toil. 7) When I called in times of trouble, You delivered me. You answered me and provided for me. 10) You are the Lord God which has brought me out of the land of Egypt (bondage). You said to me 'Open wide your mouth and I will fill it!' 13) You said if I will hearken to obey You, 14) You will subdue my enemy; and turn Your Hand against my adversary. 15) Even the wicked must bow to You and Your Power. 16) You feed me with the finest of wheat, and with honey. You satisfy all my desires!"

Stage 2: Pupa (he goes into a state of seclusion) **Rewrite the Scripture in your own handwriting.** Then meditate a few minutes on the meaning of these wonderful scriptures. This is important to help get the Word into your heart.

Stage 3: Butterfly (Maturity comes about as you let the Word work in you.) **Read, pray, or sing these verses out loud two or three times to God.** Spend at least 15 minutes each morning focusing on the goodness of God. Read each Scripture out loud and think on (ponder) what it is saying about God. It is in the taking of the Word of God into your soul that changes begin. God meant it when He said He would never leave you nor forsake you. So the only way Satan can get you and God separated is to get you to leave God. He does that by getting you hurt and feeling deserted by God. Feelings are not always the true facts. I know that can be hard to see at first. But sometimes our feelings lie to us; especially where misunderstandings are concerned. Feeling deserted does not necessarily mean you are deserted. God wants you to get to the point where you know that you know He loves you; that He is working on your

behalf and His plans for you are good. The best thing we can do for ourselves is to cooperate with God. That confidence (faith) in God opens many doors for God to bring His goodness and abundance into your life! The more you pay attention to God who loves you; the less you will hear and believe the one who hates your soul. Sing this out loud to God: I make a joyful celebration with my voice unto God. Lord, You are my Redeemer! You have brought me from the depths of my sin back into Your Presence. You have washed my sin so that it is forgotten. I shall never forget Your mercies and Your forgiveness toward me. You loved me when I was not lovely. You gave me life. You deliver my shoulder from its burden; and my hands from my toil! You said to me 'Open wide your mouth and I will fill it!' You are my strength!

Journal notes:

DAY 73

<u>Stage 1: Caterpillar</u> (remember he devours much food in preparation) First, read the Scripture to yourself.

Psalms 84:1-2, 4-7, 9-12 "How pleasant is Your House, O Lord of hosts (many)! 2) My soul longs, even faints to be in the courts of the Lord. My heart and my flesh cries out for the living God. 4) Blessed are they who dwell in Your house (in close fellowship with You). They will still be Praising You (for all eternity). 5) Blessed is the man whose strength is in You (comes from You); and whose heart is given to You (Your ways). 6) For that man who passes through a valley, makes it a well where the rain fills the pool! (Water in the bible is often showing us a picture of a lush, green and good life because water gives life to us and the earth!). 7) He has endurance and goes from strength to strength. 9) Behold, You God are our shield. Lord look upon the face of Your anointed ones. 10) One day in Your courts is better than a thousand (in prosperity in the earth). I had rather be a nothing, just a doorkeeper in Your House than to dwell with the wicked (in their riches). 11) For You God are a sun and shield (light and protection). You give grace and glory (to us). No good thing will you withhold from those who walk upright with You! 12) Blessed is the man who trusts in You!" You walk into your destiny when you heed the voice of the Holy Spirit.

<u>Stage 2: Pupa</u> (he goes into a state of seclusion) **Rewrite the Scripture in your own handwriting.** Then meditate a few minutes on the meaning of these wonderful scriptures. This is important to help get the Word into your heart.

<u>Stage 3: Butterfly</u> (Maturity comes about as you <u>let the Word work in you.</u>) **Read, pray, or sing these verses out loud two or three times to God.** Let this be your focus today: take the Scripture that speaks the most to you today and speak it all day long.

Journal notes:

DAY 74

Stage 1: Caterpillar (remember he devours much food in preparation) First, read the Scripture to yourself.

Psalms 85:1-4, 6-13 "Lord, You have been favorable to Your land and people. You have brought us out of darkness and sin's captivity. 2) You have forgiven the iniquity of Your people. You have erased my sin forever. 3) Your wrath has been removed from Your people. Your anger is forever turned away from us. 4) You have turned us back to You O God and to Your salvation. Your anger toward us is forever ceased! 6) You revive us again and cause us to rejoice in You! 7) You show us Your mercy and grant us Your salvation. 8) You speak peace to Your people. 9) Your salvation is near to any who reveres You; and Your glory will dwell in our land! (We want Your glory upon us!) 10) Mercy and truth are met together. Righteousness and peace have kissed! (God, You have brought peace into our lives with Your Righteousness.) 11) Truth will spring forth in the earth. Righteousness will see it from heaven! 12) You Lord give what is good; and cause our land to yield her increase. 13) Righteousness shall go before us; and shall set us in the way of Your steps. (Righteousness will lead us.)"

Stage 2: Pupa (he goes into a state of seclusion) **Rewrite the Scripture in your own handwriting.** Then meditate a few minutes on the meaning of these wonderful scriptures. This is important to help get the Word into your heart.

Stage 3: Butterfly (Maturity comes about as you <u>let the Word work in you.</u>) **Read, pray, or sing these verses out loud two or three times to God.** The bible continually talks of God's goodness. By now doubt should be driven from your heart; and confidence in His Love for you should be springing forth! I've noticed in my own life how the devil keeps trying to convince me that God doesn't care; and that prayer doesn't work. But as I have journeyed through these 150 days of praise, I am seeing that the devil is a liar. <u>God cares about you and me.</u> And prayer works! Sometimes things don't APPEAR to be so. But appearances are not always the truth. God is NOT at war with His people! Christ satisfied the requirements of justice on the cross. God does not require us to pay for our sins. We couldn't anyway. So mercy and truth have met and become united. That is a good thing for us because truth would condemn us, but <u>mercy stepped in and freed us</u>! Now mercy and truth are together. Righteousness and peace are also united. God is not imputing our sins to us. That was dealt with on the cross. Therefore we (born again believers) are at peace with God! Hallelujah! Let this be your focus today: take the Scripture that speaks the most to you today and speak it all day long.

Journal notes:

DAY 75

Stage 1: Caterpillar (remember he devours much food in preparation) First, read the Scripture to yourself.

Psalms 86 "Bow down Your ear O Lord and hear me for I am poor and needy. (To me that says come near and hear me O Lord. To come near speaks of intimacy. I can just see God leaning over to me to hear my words because He wants to.) 2) Preserve me Lord for I am holy (he means his hands are innocent). You are my God. Save me for I trust in (rely on) You! (I place my trust in You.) 3) Show me Your mercy for I cry to You daily. 4) Cause joy and rejoicing to bubble up for I look unto You Lord. 5) You are good; always ready to forgive; plenteous in mercy to all who call upon You. 6) I know You will give an ear to my prayers. I know You hear my cry. 7) When I am in trouble, I will call upon You; for You always hear and answer me. 8) There is no other God like You; nor any who can do Your mighty works. 9) All nations which You have made will come and worship before You, O Lord. They will glorify Your Name. 10) For You (alone) are great and mighty. You do mighty wonders. You are God alone! 11) Lord, teach me Your way. I want to walk in Your truth. Cause my heart to revere Your Name. 12) I will praise You O God with all my heart. I will glorify Your Name forever. 13) Great is Your mercy toward me. You have delivered my soul from the depths of hell. 14) My enemy rises up against me O God. 15) But You O Lord are a God full of compassion. You are gracious to me; long suffering (with my shortcomings). And You are plenteous in mercy and truth. 16) Turn unto me. Give Your strength on my behalf; for I am the child of Your servant. (I have been raised to know and worship You as my parents did.) 17) Show me a token (that You are for me) for good; that my enemy will see it, and know that You Lord help me and comfort me. They will be ashamed (and astounded). They will turn back from pursuing me when they see You are on my side!"

Stage 2: Pupa (he goes into a state of seclusion) **Rewrite the Scripture in your own handwriting.** Then meditate a few minutes on the meaning of these wonderful scriptures. This is important to help get the Word into your heart.

Stage 3: Butterfly (Maturity comes about as you <u>let the Word work in you.</u>) **Read, pray, or sing these verses out loud two or three times to God.** It is sweet and precious when a parent leans close to hear the request of their child. That intimacy is what I hear in verse 1 when it says 'bow down Your ear.' When God comes close or leans over to hear His child's request, there is intimacy. And it is beautiful. Verse 5 says God is plenteous in mercy. God's mercy is really unrecognized these days. So many people imagine that God is a God of wrath. But His heart is to show His mercy to all. Many, many scriptures talk of His mercy. He is clearly telling us that He is mercy! Let this be your focus today: take the Scripture that speaks the most to you today and speak it all day long.

Journal notes:

DAY 76

Stage 1: Caterpillar (remember he devours much food in preparation) First, read the Scripture to yourself.

Psalms 89:1-18, 28, 33-34 "I will sing of the mercies of the Lord forever. I will speak; declaring and making known Your Faithfulness to all generations. 2) Your mercy is forever. You establish Your faithfulness in the very heavens. 3) You have made a (binding) covenant with Your chosen servant - David. You have given Your Word. 4) You said his seed You will establish forever and build up his throne throughout and for all generations. 5) Lord, the heavens shall praise Your wonders; and Your faithfulness is to be praised in the congregation of the saints. 6) Who in the heaven(s) can be compared to You? Who among even the sons of the mightiest (men) can be likened to You Lord? (No one.) 7) You are to be greatly revered in the assembly of all the saints and of all who are around You. 8) O Lord God of hosts (multitude of angels); who is a strong Lord like You? Who around you is as faithful as You? 9) You (created and) rule the raging seas. You calm the waves when they are tumultuous. 10) You scatter Your enemy with Your strength. 11) The heavens are Yours; also the earth. The world and all in it are Yours for You have created and founded them. 12) You created the north and the south. The great mountains Tabor and Hermon rejoice in Your Name. 13) Mighty is Your arm, O God! Strong is Your Hand. High (Just) is Your right Hand. 14) Justice and true judgment are in Your throne. Mercy and truth always go before Your face. 15) Blessed are the people who know the joyful sound (of You). They shall walk O Lord, in the light of Your Face and Your Spirit. 16) We shall rejoice in Your Name all the day (for Your Name sustains us). In Your Righteousness we shall be exalted. 17) For You are the glory of our strength. In Your favor our lives shall be (covered and) lifted up above our enemies! 18) For You, Lord are our defense. The Holy One of Israel is our King! 28) Your mercy is with us forever. You make Your covenant to stand fast (unmovable, unbreakable). 33) Your faithfulness never fails. 34) <u>God, You said Your covenant You will not break; nor alter the Words which have gone out of Your mouth!</u>"

Stage 2: Pupa (he goes into a state of seclusion) **Rewrite the Scripture in your own handwriting.** Then meditate a few minutes on the meaning of these wonderful scriptures. This is important to help get the Word into your heart.

Stage 3: Butterfly (Maturity comes about as you <u>let the Word work in you.</u>) **Read, pray, or sing these verses out loud two or three times to God.** Just think a minute about verse 14. It lists 4 things that are always with God - 1) Justice-that means God will cause justice to come to you. Just trust Him to do so. 2) True Judgment-Don't worry about other people (wicked) getting their just rewards. You just keep your own heart open and pure before the Lord for He sees all and He will deal with all. 3) Mercy-Be always thankful that our God is a God of mercy. We all need mercy. If God had no mercy in Him, we would all be dead and in hell. 4) Truth-God is absolute truth as well as just and merciful. He cannot even lie. If He declares a thing, it will be. We can not put a time limit on Him for it to come to pass. I don't know about you, but it comforts me a great deal to know God is these 4 things-justice, judgment, mercy, and truth! How powerful is this; God, You said that 'Your covenant You will not break, nor alter the thing which has gone out of Your mouth!' We break our word coming and going these days. But God never breaks His Word when He has given it. Hallelujah! And a covenant to Him is a binding thing forever. Because God is in covenant with us, He will not let His children down! Let this be your focus today: take the Scripture that speaks the most to you today and speak it all day long.

Journal notes:

DAY 77

Stage 1: Caterpillar (remember he devours much food in preparation) First, read the Scripture to yourself.

Psalms 90:1-3, 12, 14, 16-17 "Lord, You have been our dwelling place for all generations. 2) Before the mountains were brought forth (from the depths of the sea); before You had formed the earth and the world; from everlasting to everlasting YOU ARE GOD! 3) You turn man and tell him to repent and return to You. 12) Teach us to number (realize the shortness of) our days (here on earth) and to value our life; that we may apply our hearts to wisdom. 14) You satisfy us with Your mercy that we may rejoice and be glad all the days of our lives. (Thank You for Your mercy on us.) 16) You reveal Your workings unto us. Your glory is revealed to our children. Let Your glory be seen upon our children. 17) Let Your beauty be upon us. Establish Thou the work of our hands. You establish the work of our hands O Lord."

Stage 2: Pupa (he goes into a state of seclusion) **Rewrite the Scripture in your own handwriting.** Then meditate a few minutes on the meaning of these wonderful scriptures. This is important to help get the Word into your heart.

Stage 3: Butterfly (Maturity comes about as you let the Word work in you.) **Read, pray, or sing these verses out loud two or three times to God.** We are just beyond the halfway mark now. And I have begun to see a change in the way I pray to God. My attitude now in praying is totally different. Now instead of acting as if my problems were huge; when I make a request, I know God is far bigger than any problem I may have. So I come to God in confidence that He hears me; that He cares about me; and that He will answer. He will take care of the situation and nothing that troubles me is bigger than Him. One of the things which have stood out in my mind thus far is how often the scriptures talk about God's mercy! He wants us to know He is mercy! These scriptures every morning that I say out loud to God are also my

confessions throughout the day. They keep my mind on God's faithfulness; for He is a good God! Let this be your focus today: take the Scripture that speaks the most to you today and speak it all day long.

Journal notes:

DAY 78

Stage 1: Caterpillar (remember he devours much food in preparation) First, read the Scripture to yourself.

Psalms 91 "He who dwells in the secret place (that's me) of the most High shall abide (live) under the shadow (protection) of the Almighty! 2) I will say of the Lord, You are my refuge. Lord, You are my fortress. Lord, You are my God. In You I will (place my) trust. 3) Surely (of a surety) You deliver me from the trap of the trapper; and from the noisome pestilence (deadly diseases). 4) You cover me with Your feathers (protection). Under Your wings (covering) I shall trust (and be safe). Your truth will be my shield and buckle. (Your truth will protect and guard me from lies of the enemy.) 5) I will not fear the terrors of the night; nor the dangers in the day. 6) I will not fear the pestilence that walks in darkness (seeking whom it may devour). I will not fear the destruction that destroys and lays waste in the midday. 7) Though a thousand fall at one side and ten thousand at my right side; it shall not come near me (or my family)! (Glory to God!) 8) Only with my eyes shall I see the fall/reward of the wicked, 9) because I have made/ I make the Lord my place of refuge. I make the most High God my place of habitation (where I dwell always). 10) So there shall no evil befall me. Neither shall plagues come near my dwelling place. 11) For God has given His angels charge over me; to (protect and) keep me everywhere I go. 12) They shall bear me up in their hands, lest any danger come to me. 13) I shall tread upon the lion and snake to trample them under my feet. **14) God has declared this over me: God said to me that because I have set my love on Him; therefore He will deliver me. God will set me on high. This is because I have known His Holy Name. 15) When I call upon God; He will answer. God will be with me when I have trouble. And God has promised to deliver me. God will bring me into a place of honor. 16) With long life God will satisfy my soul. God will show me His Salvation!"**

Stage 2: Pupa (he goes into a state of seclusion) **In the space below, rewrite the agreement in verses 14-16.**

Stage 3: Butterfly (Maturity comes about as you <u>let the Word work in you.</u>) Shout for joy because God declares these things over any who 'set their love toward Him' (verse 14). Any who set their face to seek Him will be: 1) rewarded with long life fully satisfied; 2)given honor; 3)given a protective covering of God and deliverance in trouble; 4)placed in authority; 5)God will hear when you call and He will answer! He will do a lot just for us to set our face and heart to love Him. Many people these days fear a lot of things: loss of job, loss of family, loss of home, loss of life itself. But God says to all of that - just turn to Me. Don't seek worldly things. Seek Me; and I will give you all you need, plus a long and satisfied life! (Matt 6:33) God makes our way prosperous when He becomes the focus of our life! We mustn't seek to hold on to things that won't matter in eternity; while we ignore the things that do! Make this agreement part of your life by reciting it frequently; especially in times of trouble or need.

Journal notes:

DAY 79

<u>Stage 1: Caterpillar</u> (remember he devours much food in preparation) First, read the Scripture to yourself.

Psalms 92 "It is good to give thanks to the Lord. I sing praises unto Your Name O Most High, 2) to show forth (speak about) Your loving kindness in the morning, and Your faithfulness every night. 3) I will praise You with instruments of music. 4) For You, O Lord have made me glad through the works of Your Hands. I triumph and glory in the works of Your Hands. 5) O Lord how great and mighty are Your Works; and Your thoughts are too deep (amazing) for me! 6) The wicked and foolish do not understand at all. 7) They may flourish for a short time, but they will be destroyed forever. 8) But You, O Lord, Most High God are forever. 9) My enemies will perish; all evil workers will be dealt with. 10) **I shall be exalted by You. I shall be anointed with fresh oil.** 11) I will see the wicked go down. 12) But the righteous shall flourish like the palm tree. He shall grow like the strong, tall cedar. 13) Those who are planted in the house of God shall flourish in His courts. 14) They shall still produce fruit even in old age. They shall be blessed and flourishing. 15) To show that the Lord is upright. (He brings justice to the righteous.) Lord, You are my rock. There is no unrighteousness in You!"

<u>Stage 2: Pupa</u> (he goes into a state of seclusion) **Rewrite the Scripture in your own handwriting.** Then meditate a few minutes on the meaning of these wonderful scriptures. This is important to help get the Word into your heart.

<u>Stage 3: Butterfly</u> (Maturity comes about as you <u>let the Word work in you.</u>) **Read, pray, or sing these verses out loud two or three times to God.** Daily take the time to speak these praises out to God. Allow the Word to work in your heart. Let praise take over your mind continually and you will begin to see God's Hand over you in every situation in your life. Sit for a few moments in total quiet and say verse 10 over and over. 'I will be exalted by You God. I will be anointed with a fresh touch of the Holy Spirit.' It is amazing how much joy we can get by focusing on God and His power; on His Love for us; and on His goodness rather than the terrible deeds of the wicked and their

leader, Satan. God is so much more powerful than any evil demon. And He is good, kind and loving. He has good plans for us as Jeremiah 29:11-13 tells us. Jeremiah 29:11-13 "For I know the thoughts I think toward you, saith the Lord (to you). (I have) thoughts of peace, not of evil (or harm); (plans) to give you an expected (good) end (of days). 12) You shall call upon Me. You shall go and pray to Me; and I will hear you and answer you! 13) You shall seek Me, and (you will) find Me when you search for Me with your whole heart!" Let this be your focus today: take the Scripture that speaks the most to you today and speak it all day long.

Journal notes:

DAY 80

Stage 1: Caterpillar (remember he devours much food in preparation) First, read the Scripture to yourself.

Psalms 93 "The Lord reigns. Lord, You are clothed with majesty, (beauty of holiness). You are clothed with (might and) strength. You have girded (clothed) Yourself with strength. You established the world that it cannot be moved. 2) Your throne is established of old. You are from everlasting (to everlasting). (You always were and always shall be!) 3) The floods have lifted up, O Lord. The floods have lifted up their voice (to You)! 4) For You Lord are on High and mightier than the noise of many waters; mightier than the waves of the sea. 5) Your testimony (Word) is sure (a solid foundation; an unmovable, unchangeable rock). Lord, holiness decorates (beautifies) Your House forever."

Psalms 95: 1-7 "O come let us sing unto the Lord. Let us make a joyful noise to the rock of our salvation. 2) **Let us come before Your Presence with thanksgiving.** Let us make a joyful noise unto Him with psalms. 3) For You Lord are a great God, and a great King above all gods. 4) In Your Hand are the deep places of the earth. The strength of the hills also is Yours. 5) The sea is Yours for You made it. Your Hands formed the dry land. 6) O come, we shall worship and bow down. We shall kneel before the Lord our Maker. 7) For You are our God. We are the people of Your pasture, and the sheep of Your Hand."

Stage 2: Pupa (he goes into a state of seclusion) **Rewrite the Scripture in your own handwriting.** Then meditate a few minutes on the meaning of these wonderful scriptures. This is important to help get the Word into your heart.

Stage 3: Butterfly (Maturity comes about as you let the Word work in you.) **Read, pray, or sing these verses out loud two or three times to God.** Psalms 95:2 to me shows that an attitude of praise is the attitude God wants to see on us. To present yourself before royalty is to present your best side as respect. How much more should we have an attitude of praise when we come before the God of the universe! Let this be your focus today: take the Scripture that speaks the most to you today and speak it all day long.

Journal notes:

DAY 81

Stage 1: Caterpillar (remember he devours much food in preparation) First, read the Scripture to yourself.

Psalms 96 "O sing unto the Lord a new song. Sing unto the Lord, all the earth. 2) Sing unto the Lord. Bless His Holy Name. Show forth His Salvation day after day. 3) Declare His Glory among the heathen; and declare (tell about) His wonders among all people. 4) For You (alone) Lord are great; and greatly to be praised. 5) All the gods of the heathen are but idols; but You Lord made the heavens. 6) Honor and majesty are before You. Strength and beauty are in Your sanctuary. 7) Give unto the Lord, ye people, give glory and strength (due His Name). (Praise God for His Glory and strength.) 8) Give unto the Lord the glory due His Name. Bring an offering and come into His courts (in Praise). 9) Worship the Lord in the beauty of holiness. Fear before Him, all the earth. 10) Say among the heathen that the Lord reigns. The world shall be established; it shall not be moved. The Lord will judge the people in righteousness. 11) Let the heavens (sing out and) rejoice! Let the earth be glad. Let the sea roar and the fullness of it (roar also). 12) Let the fields be joyful and all that is in it. Then the trees of the woods shall rejoice 13) before the Lord. For You come. You come to judge the earth. You shall judge the world with (Your) Righteousness; and (judge) the people with Your truth!"

Stage 2: Pupa (he goes into a state of seclusion) **Rewrite the Scripture in your own handwriting.** Then meditate a few minutes on the meaning of these wonderful scriptures. This is important to help get the Word into your heart.

Stage 3: Butterfly (Maturity comes about as you <u>let the Word work in you.</u>) **Read, pray, or sing these verses out loud two or three times to God.** Verse 8 says bring an offering and come into His courts with praise. I thought about that for a minute. What could I possibly give God? He owns it all. Then I saw that **God wants me. He wants my heart and life.** There is no offering more precious to Him than when we give Him all we have - ourselves; our whole heart and life. After all He has done for us, for me, it is a minor gift/ offering. No gift I can give Him can compare to the gift Jesus has given me.

Jesus suffered horribly in order to gain us. We were bought back from sin's dreadful clutches. He paid a high price for my soul so that I would not have to go to hell with my sins. I cannot give enough to make up for that! But I can give all that I am in thankful appreciation that the God who made the universe loves me that much! Too many do not know how much God loves them. We too were once in darkness of sin; desperately looking for love. Yet He was there all along, calling us to Himself. He is the Love we need! Let His love for you become your focus today.

Journal notes:

DAY 82

Stage 1: Caterpillar (remember he devours much food in preparation) First, read the Scripture to yourself.

Psalms 97 "The Lord reigns. Let (all) the earth rejoice. Let the multitude of islands be glad (that the Lord reigns)! 2) Righteousness and justice inhabit Your throne. 3) A fire goes before You and burns up Your enemies round about! 4) Your lightning enlightens the world. The earth sees and trembles (in fear and reverence, for Your power is so awesome and mighty)! 5) The hills melt like wax in the Presence of the Lord! 6) The heavens declare Your Righteousness. All the people will see Your Glory! 7) Those who worship idols will be confused. Worship the Lord instead. 8) Zion heard, and was glad. The daughters of Judah rejoiced because of Your Judgments, O Lord. 9) For You, O Lord, are High above all the earth. You are exalted far above all gods. 10) Those who love the Lord hate evil. Lord, You preserve the souls of Your saints. You deliver us from the hand of the wicked. 11) Light is given to the righteous. Gladness is given to the upright in heart! 12) All ye righteous rejoice in the Lord. We give thanks at the remembrance of Your Holiness!"

Stage 2: Pupa (he goes into a state of seclusion) **Rewrite the Scripture in your own handwriting.** Then meditate a few minutes on the meaning of these wonderful scriptures. This is important to help get the Word into your heart.

Stage 3: Butterfly (Maturity comes about as you <u>let the Word work in you.</u>) **Read, pray, or sing these verses out loud two or three times to God.** Verse 2 is saying what God is. He is a righteous and just judge. The throne represents the highest authority available. If the highest authority available to you is righteous, just and fair; then you do not have to worry about getting justice! You may be like me, and struggle in this area because you have been done wrong so much and have seen so little justice in the world. Yet God never fails to correct a matter. When it takes a long time for justice, it is usually because we have not given it to Him to correct; and left it there. We may be trying to get justice for ourselves. That never works. So we may be hindering

the process of justice by not allowing God to deal with it. That shows we don't truly trust God. God is not a man. Justice is who He is. Let's decide today we will begin forgiving people and leaving recompense in God's Hands. He will handle it. Whenever you struggle with what someone has done, just say over and over out loud to yourself: 'God's throne is justice. I am innocent in this matter.' (Be sure that you are innocent. No talking ugly about the person behind their back or continually reciting the offense. This makes you guilty too and causes God to have to deal with you also. It steals your joy, and prolongs justice!) Verse 1 says 'The Lord reigns.' God is the ultimate power! No one else has a greater power than our God! Everything and everyone else who is alive has been created by God, by His Spirit and by Jesus (the Word of God)! So God is the ultimate power – and He is Righteous. His judgments are just! We could've been stuck with the ultimate power being evil. But we aren't! <u>Our God is the God</u> and He is love, truth and justice. Knowing that should dispel all fear! Verse 11 says "Gladness is given to the upright in heart.' Unforgiveness in your heart overrides joy. Any who choose to forgive even when it is very hard will be rewarded with gladness, joy, peace, and happiness; while those who hang onto unforgiveness will have all their joy stolen. Peace is very necessary these days. Just remember God is just. He will make restitution when we leave recompense in His Hands! Let this be your focus today: take the Scripture that speaks the most to you today and speak it all day long.

Journal notes:

DAY 83

Stage 1: Caterpillar (remember he devours much food in preparation) First, read the Scripture to yourself.

Psalms 98 "O, I sing unto You Lord with a new song, for You have done marvelous things. Your right Hand and Your Holy Arm have gotten You the victory! 2) You have made known Your salvation. You have openly shown Your Righteousness (to us) in the sight of the heathen. 3) You have remembered Your Mercy and Your truth toward the house (nation) of Israel (and me). All the ends of the earth have seen (been eye witness to) the salvation of (coming from) our God! 4) (Therefore I will) make a joyful noise unto the Lord. All the earth, make a loud noise; rejoice and sing praise(s) (to our God and King). 5) Sing unto the Lord with a harp and (let your) voice (praise Him) with a psalm. 6) With all kinds of musical instruments make a joyful noise before the Lord our King! 7) Let the seas roar and the fullness thereof; the whole world and all who dwell in it. 8) Let the floods clap hands. Let the hills be joyful together 9) before the Lord for He comes to judge the earth with justice. He shall judge the world with (His) Righteousness and the people with equity (bringing fairness)!"

Stage 2: Pupa (he goes into a state of seclusion) **Rewrite the Scripture in your own handwriting.** Then meditate a few minutes on the meaning of these wonderful scriptures. This is important to help get the Word into your heart.

Stage 3: Butterfly (Maturity comes about as you <u>let the Word work in you.</u>) **Read, pray, or sing these verses out loud two or three times to God.** If that isn't upbeat I don't know what is. Verse 3 says all the ends of the earth will be an eye witness to the salvation of (from) our God! They will not be able to deny that God is the God! Verses 7-8 gives a description of so much joy and praise going on that even the land and seas begin to praise Him! Just imagine that much praise going on in the earth and rising up to heaven! Verse 4 says to get loud and make a lot of praise noise. This is not describing a quiet little timid voice that is whispering 'I love You Lord.' No! This is a description of our praise being bold and loud. **There is nothing wrong with loud praise.**

Of course the Holy Spirit will direct you when and where. But do not be ashamed of praising God. You don't see shyness at a ball game when someone feels like clapping or shouting hooray. Let joy bubble up within you and overflow. Let it come out of your mouth with zeal and energy. God deserves so much more praise than we give Him. Verse 1 says 'I sing unto You Lord... for You have done marvelous things.' From creating us to saving us to daily loving and caring for us; we have a million and one things to be thankful for. But our minds seem to stay on what is going wrong in our lives instead of on praising God for these million and one things that He has blessed us with! All day today focus on your own reasons for praising Him! Throughout these 150 days of praise, you will find your heart changing toward God!

Journal notes:

DAY 84

Stage 1: Caterpillar (remember he devours much food in preparation) First, read the Scripture to yourself.

Psalms 99 "The Lord reigns. Let the people respect Him. He is enthroned between the cherubim (on the mercy seat). 2) The Lord is great (mighty) in Zion. He is to be exalted above all. 3) We will praise Your Great and Mighty Name, for it is Holy! 4) You establish equity, truth, justice and righteousness in Your chosen people. 5) We exalt You O Lord our God. We worship at Your feet, God, for You are Holy. 6) When Moses and Aaron called upon Your Name, You answered them. 7) You spoke to them out of a cloud. They kept the ordinances You gave them (because they loved You). 8) You forgave them their iniquities. 9) We exalt You O Lord our God. We worship at Your Holy Mountain (where Your Presence is); for You are Holy!"

Stage 2: Pupa (he goes into a state of seclusion) **Rewrite the Scripture in your own handwriting.** Then meditate a few minutes on the meaning of these wonderful scriptures. This is important to help get the Word into your heart.

Stage 3: Butterfly (Maturity comes about as you <u>let the Word work in you.</u>) **Read, pray, or sing these verses out loud two or three times to God.** These verses speak to me about the holiness of God; and the reverential fear and respect we are to keep in our hearts toward Him. This is not of course saying God is horrible and to be feared. God is holy though, and to be revered. Many of the generation born from 1990 on have not been taught to respect their elders or God. A reverential fear is healthy. Losing awe and respect for God is a terrible place to be. But it is easy to return to it by reading about His Power, His Might and His Love for us. He is Holy and He will deal with evil permanently on Judgment Day. Until then He has granted us a time of mercy for us to turn back to Him while there is breath in our body. The time

is now. We must practice worshipping at His feet and knowing in our hearts that HE IS GOD! Let this be your focus today: take the Scripture that speaks the most to you today and speak it all day long.

Journal notes:

DAY 85

Stage 1: Caterpillar (remember he devours much food in preparation) First, read the Scripture to yourself.

Psalms 100 "Make a joyful noise unto the Lord, all ye lands. 2) Serve the Lord with gladness. Come before His Presence with singing (not grumbling! 3) Know ye that the Lord, He is God. It is He that has made us, and not we ourselves. We are His people, and the sheep of His pasture. 4) Enter into His gates with thanksgiving; and into His courts with praise! Be thankful unto Him and bless His Holy Name. 5) For the Lord is good. His mercy is everlasting. His truth is to all generations!"

Stage 2: Pupa (he goes into a state of seclusion) **Rewrite the Scripture in your own handwriting.** Then meditate a few minutes on the meaning of these wonderful scriptures. This is important to help get the Word into your heart.

Stage 3: Butterfly (Maturity comes about as you <u>let the Word work in you.</u>) **Read, pray, or sing these verses out loud two or three times to God.** Remember the more time you spend on each devotional, the more you will get out of it; and the quicker you will see breakthroughs! Envision yourself walking into the outer gates of God's throne. Let a humble and thankful spirit envelope you. Thank Him for all you have! After a few minutes in the outer court - come into His throne room. It's OK, you're always welcome. As you come into His Holy Presence, let praise for Him fill your heart. Let it come forth out of your mouth. Praise Him because He is God; and a good God. He is holy. Let praise pour forth. It is a good cleansing effect. The more you praise Him, the more He can erase things like fear, anger and unforgiveness from your life! Place them (fear, anger, and unforgiveness) on the altar. Ask God to purge you of them. After a few moments just kneel before God and be silent. Allow God to speak to your heart. As you go about your business today, spiritually stay before the throne of God.

Journal notes:

DAY 86

Stage 1: Caterpillar (remember he devours much food in preparation) First, read the Scripture to yourself.

Psalms 101:1: "I will sing of Your mercy and Your justice forever. Unto You, O Lord, will I sing!"

Psalms 102:12-21 "You, O Lord shall endure forever. Your remembrance is unto all generations. 13) You shall arise, having mercy on Zion. **For the time to favor Zion; the set time is come (now)!** 14) The servants of the Lord find pleasure in Zion's stones (and beauty). 15) The heathen (wicked) shall fear (revere) the Name of the Lord. All the kings of the earth revere Your Glory, Lord! 16) When You Lord build up Zion, You shall appear in all Your Glory! 17) You will hear and regard (respond to) the prayer of the destitute (and lonely). 18) This is written for the generations to come; the people which shall praise the Lord! 19) For You O Lord have looked down from Your sanctuary. From heaven You beheld (looked upon) the earth. 20) You heard the groaning of the prisoner. (You came) to loose (free) those appointed unto death. 21) We (shall) declare Your Name in Zion. We declare Your praise in the holy city Jerusalem."

Stage 2: Pupa (he goes into a state of seclusion) **Rewrite the Scripture in your own handwriting.** Then meditate a few minutes on the meaning of these wonderful scriptures. This is important to help get the Word into your heart.

Stage 3: Butterfly (Maturity comes about as you <u>let the Word work in you.</u>) **Read, pray, or sing these verses out loud two or three times to God.** I woke up this morning and right away I began praising God. Everyone will have issues in this life. If we wait until everything is perfect before we praise Him, there will be no praise. And nothing in our life would change. In the famous story of Joshua marching around Jericho and the walls falling, they never lifted a hammer against the walls. On the 7th day, as they marched around the wall, their praise was so loud, the wall fell like a house made of

cardboard; simply from praising! The Israelites didn't wait until the walls fell before they praised God. They shouted praises and sang to God first. Then the walls hindering them fell. Think about that! Praise always precedes the victory because victory rides in on praise; while grumbling, anger and resentment keep us in our dilemmas and they prevent God from moving on our behalf. Practicing praise builds up our faith. Then faith opens the door and lets God work on our behalf. **Praise is vital to us winning the victory in our lives.** The devil is not meant to win nor destroy us. We are the ones who give Satan an in-road (open door) by our grumbling, etc. Today, every time you catch yourself grumbling, turn it into praise!

Journal notes:

DAY 87

Stage 1: Caterpillar (remember he devours much food in preparation) First, read the Scripture to yourself.

Psalms 103 "Bless the Lord oh my soul, and all that is within me, bless Your Holy Name. 2) Bless the Lord, oh my soul. I shall not forget all Your benefits (blessings). 3) For You forgive all my iniquities. You heal all my diseases. 4) You redeemed my life from destruction. You crowned me with Your loving kindness and tender mercies. 5) You satisfy my mouth with good, so my youth is renewed like the eagle's. 6) You execute righteousness and justice for all who are oppressed. 7) You made known Your ways unto Moses; and Your acts (power was revealed) to the people of Israel. 8) Lord, You are merciful and gracious. You are slow to anger and plenteous in mercy. 9) You will not always rebuke us; neither will You keep Your anger forever! (Thank goodness!) 10) (In fact) You have not dealt with us (as we deserved) according to our sins; nor have You given us our just desserts for those sins. (Again You are full of mercy which we do not deserve!) 11) For as high as the heavens are over the earth, so great is Your mercy toward those who love and revere You! (That's a powerful lot of mercy!) 12) You have also removed (permanently) our sins from us as far as the east is from the west! (That one thrills me because I never want to be associated with my sins again!) 13) You've had pity on us like a father pities his children. (There is an emotional bond between us like father and child.) 14) You know our frailties and our weaknesses. 15) You will remember that we flourish today 16) and in a very short time, we pass from this life. 17) So though this life is ended in a short time span; yet Your mercy O Lord is from everlasting to everlasting for those who revere and love You. (His mercy always has been; and there is no end to it.) Your righteousness (which we do not deserve) is passed down to our children and our grandchildren."

Stage 2: Pupa (he goes into a state of seclusion) **Rewrite the Scripture in your own handwriting.** Then meditate a few minutes on the meaning of these wonderful scriptures. This is important to help get the Word into your heart.

Stage 3: Butterfly (Maturity comes about as you <u>let the Word work in you.</u>)
Read, pray, or sing these verses out loud two or three times to God. We do not speak these praises out loud to God for Him to hear them. He already knows these things. We need to hear how awesome He is. We need to hear that He is faithful. And we need to hear ourselves say it in order to really believe it. Praise to God is for our benefit; not so God can hear how great He is. We are the ones who need our heart strengthened with faith in God (and in His love for us)! That faith comes by hearing His Word come out of our mouth! Romans 10:10 is often used as a salvation verse. But it is much more than that. Rom 10:10 "...with the heart man believes (and comes) into (God's) righteousness; with the mouth (out loud) confession is made (creates) salvation. (This is not just being born again. It is also healing, prosperity, etc.) As the heart believes and the mouth speaks, faith arises inside the spirit of man and salvation is created by the power of God. This brings healing, prosperity and all that God promises to us in His Word. Speak His Word. Let faith arise and our enemies (sickness, lack, unforgiveness) be scattered! Verse 2 says I shall not forget all Your benefits (blessings). Then the next 15 verses lists those benefits! Thank Him for some of them today!

Journal notes:

DAY 88

Stage 1: Caterpillar (remember he devours much food in preparation) First, read the Scripture to yourself.

Psalms 104: 1-7, 9-11, 14, 16-19, 21, 24, 31, 33-35 "Bless the Lord, O my soul. O Lord my God, You are very great. You are clothed with honor and majesty. 2) You cover Yourself with light as with a garment. You stretched out the heavens like a curtain. 3) You laid the beams of Your chambers in the waters. You make the clouds Your chariot. You walk upon the wings of the wind. 4) You make Your angels spirits, ministers in a flaming fire. 5) You lay the foundations of the earth that it should not be removed forever. 6) You covered the earth with the deep ocean. The waters stood above the mountains. 7) At Your rebuke they fled. 9) You set the boundaries that the ocean could not pass. 10) You send springs into the hills 11) to give drink to every beast. 14) You cause grass to grow for man and beast. 16) Your trees are full and beautiful. 17) You provided homes in the trees for all birds. 18) The hills and rocks are home for goats and conies. 19) You appointed the moon for seasons. The sun was designated a time to rise and a time to set. 21) You feed all the animals. 24) Oh Lord, how many and how glorious are Your Works. By Your Wisdom all was created. The earth is full of and creation reflects Your Glory! 31) The Glory of the Lord endures forever. The Lord is pleased with the works of His Hands. 33) I will sing unto the Lord as long as I live! I will sing praise to my God while I have breath in my body. 34) My meditation of You shall be sweet. I will be glad in the Lord. 35) Bless the Lord, oh my soul. Praise the Lord (for He is a mighty God)!"

Stage 2: Pupa (he goes into a state of seclusion) **Rewrite the Scripture in your own handwriting.** Then meditate a few minutes on the meaning of these wonderful scriptures. This is important to help get the Word into your heart.

Stage 3: Butterfly (Maturity comes about as you <u>let the Word work in you.</u>)
Read, pray, or sing these verses out loud two or three times to God. Part of being in awe of God is to look at all of creation and be amazed at a God who can create it all! Let this be your focus today: take the Scripture that speaks the most to you today and speak it all day long.

Journal notes:

DAY 89

Stage 1: Caterpillar (remember he devours much food in preparation) First, read the Scripture to yourself.

Psalms 105: 1-8, 15, 37, 44-45 "Oh (I) give thanks unto the Lord. I call upon Your Name, Lord. I declare Your mighty works among the people. 2) I sing psalms unto You. I shall speak of all Your wondrous works! 3) I will glory in Your Holy Name. Let my heart rejoice as I seek You. 4) I will seek You Lord and Your Might. I will seek Your Face forevermore. 5) I remember Your marvelous works (for me) which You have done; all Your wonders and the justice that comes from Your mouth. 6) I am the seed of Abraham (the servant of God); and I am of Jacob, God's chosen. (Therefore I am of the blessed and the chosen!) 7)You are the Lord my God. Your justice is in the earth! 8) You have not forgotten Your covenant; for You commanded it to go to a thousand generations (this includes me)! 15) Over Israel and me You have declared - 'Touch not Mine anointed; and do My prophets no harm.' With great signs and wonders You brought Your people out of Egyptian bondage. 37) Furthermore You brought them out as You do us with much wealth and with not one sick or feeble! 44) You provided for them and us in the desert; then gave them the lands of the heathen. We inherit all the wicked have labored for. 45) We will observe Your laws to keep them. Praise Your mighty and Holy Name Lord!"

Stage 2: Pupa (he goes into a state of seclusion) **Rewrite the Scripture in your own handwriting.** Then meditate a few minutes on the meaning of these wonderful scriptures. This is important to help get the Word into your heart.

Stage 3: Butterfly (Maturity comes about as you <u>let the Word work in you.</u>) **Read, pray, or sing these verses out loud two or three times to God.** Not only did God bring Israel out of bondage, but He is still faithful today. God is still healing, restoring families, providing for our needs and breaking darkness off! Our God is so good. There are quite a few promises in this chapter we can believe God to bring about in our lives. We do so by declaring them out

loud over and over and over. They will settle deep in our heart and mind; bringing us the victory we need: 1) Verse 6: I am blessed and chosen! 2) Verse 15: Over Israel and me God, You declared: 'Touch not My anointed; do My prophets no harm. Therefore I declare I have supernatural protection of God from heaven! 3) Verse 37: God brings me out of bondage with health and great wealth! 4) Verse 44: We inherit the lands of the heathen; and all the wicked have labored for! Start cultivating the promises of God in your heart today.

Journal notes:

DAY 90

<u>Stage 1: Caterpillar</u> (remember he devours much food in preparation) First, read the Scripture to yourself.

Psalms 106 "I praise You Lord. I give thanks unto You for You are good; Your mercy endures forever."

Psalms 107:1-3, 8-16, 20 "I give thanks unto You Lord, for You are good; Your mercy endures forever. 2) Let the redeemed of the Lord say so; for You Lord have redeemed me from the enemy's hand (many times). 3) You gather Your people back unto You; bringing them from the east, west, north and south. 8) Oh that men would praise You Lord for Your goodness and for Your wonderful works to us. 9) You satisfy the longing soul; You fill the hungry soul with goodness. 10) When we sat in darkness and in the shadow of death, bound in affliction by Satan, 11) it was because of our rebellion. We rebelled against Your Word God and disrespected the Word and Presence of the Most High God. 12) Therefore we were bound in sin (and darkness). 13) Yet when we cried out to You Lord, You saved us from our distresses. **14) You brought me out of the darkness and You broke the chains that had bound me! 15) Oh God I praise You for Your goodness and mercy; and Your wonderful works to me. 16) You have broken the gates of brass and cut the iron that had bound me. (You brought me out of my dungeon of darkness. You freed me from the prison Satan had me bound in. I am set free because You had mercy on me! You are a good God! I am free; I am free! I will love You and serve You forever because You love me! 20) Then You sent Your Word and healed me and delivered me from the destruction Satan had prepared for me. (God, You are so good to me!)**"

<u>Stage 2: Pupa</u> (he goes into a state of seclusion) **Rewrite the Scripture in your own handwriting.** Then meditate a few minutes on the meaning of these wonderful scriptures. This is important to help get the Word into your heart.

Stage 3: Butterfly (Maturity comes about as you <u>let the Word work in you.</u>) **Read, pray, or sing these verses out loud two or three times to God.** Although many sins and their terrible results are things we have stepped into ourselves; yet God has mercy on us because He loves us. And He wants to redeem us and restore us to our original position as kings and queens under Him. He desires to pour out His many blessings upon us. Though I was in darkness now I am free because God had mercy on me! Therefore from here on I choose to love, obey and follow God. Today meditate on verses 14 - 16, declaring them out loud all day long. I am free for God has mercy on me!

Journal notes:

DAY 91

<u>Stage 1: Caterpillar</u> (remember he devours much food in preparation) First, read the Scripture to yourself.

Psalms 107:21-24, 28, 31, 35-38, 41-43 "Oh how I shall praise You Lord for Your goodness; and for Your wonderful works to man. 22) I will give the sacrifices of thanksgiving! I shall declare Your works with rejoicing! 23) Men who go down to the sea in great ships 24) see Your mighty works 28) for when they cry to You in their trouble, You bring them out of their distresses! 31) O how I shall Praise You Lord for Your goodness! 35) You turn the wilderness into standing water; and (You turn) dry ground into water springs (for us)! 36) There You prepare a city for those without a home and food for the hungry! 37) There the fields are sown with food; vineyards and fruit trees give their fruit. 38) You bless it all so it is multiplied greatly! 41) You set the poor on high from affliction; and cause him to have abundance of family! 42) The righteous rejoice. 43) The wise understand and see it is the loving kindness of the Lord (that does these things)!"

<u>Stage 2: Pupa</u> (he goes into a state of seclusion) **Rewrite the Scripture in your own handwriting.** Then meditate a few minutes on the meaning of these wonderful scriptures. This is important to help get the Word into your heart.

<u>Stage 3: Butterfly</u> (Maturity comes about as you <u>let the Word work in you.</u>) **Read, pray, or sing these verses out loud two or three times to God.** I've always liked verse 35 because it is very descriptive of how God can turn our life of wilderness (where there is no beauty, nothing good growing, no hope or joy) into a lush, healthy life. Water in the bible often represents the giving of life because in nature water is vital to life. No life would exist without water. Water makes things lush and beautiful. So we could use verse 35 as a promise from God for a lush, good and beautiful life. If we have no hope and cannot envision a good life; then we need to spend a great deal of time just worshipping at God's feet. That is where hope comes alive again - in pure worship of God - not asking Him for anything. Close your eyes and

just worship God and meditate on His goodness awhile! These scriptures list at least 4 things to be thankful for: God's goodness, His blessings, His protection and His provision. Meditate on some of those today and keep your heart in a spirit of thankfulness and praise.

Journal notes:

DAY 92

Stage 1: Caterpillar (remember he devours much food in preparation) First, read the Scripture to yourself.

Psalms 108:1-6 "Oh God, my heart is fixed. I will sing and give praise, even my glory. 2) Awake psaltery and harp. I will awake early (eager to praise You Lord)! 3) I will praise You O Lord among the people. I will sing praises among the nations! 4) For Your mercy is great above the heavens (higher than the heavens). Your truth reaches to the clouds. 5) Be thou exalted O God above the heavens. **Let Your Glory be above (over) all the earth!** 6) That Your beloved may be delivered; for You save with Your right hand and answer me."

Stage 2: Pupa (he goes into a state of seclusion) **Rewrite the Scripture in your own handwriting.** Then meditate a few minutes on the meaning of these wonderful scriptures. This is important to help get the Word into your heart.

Stage 3: Butterfly (Maturity comes about as you <u>let the Word work in you.</u>) **Read, pray, or sing these verses out loud two or three times to God.** I believe we really fail to recognize just how much mercy God has toward us. It is humbling to realize we really do not deserve His mercy. Part of learning awe for God is recognizing the difference between Him and us. He is Creator. We're created by Him. He is so Holy we cannot even fathom it all; yet He wants us to be with Him! He is so powerful He has only to speak and all things must respond to Him! He always has been and forever will be. Many call Him Ancient of Days. He is God, who created heaven and earth; and yet He has mercy on us. (Think about that!) God is love and mercy, truth and righteousness. Be Thou exalted O God. Let Your Glory be above all the earth. We are not to focus on our needs in this world. We are to pray about them; but then we are to focus on our God who is mightier than any need we'll ever have! We are to jump and shout for joy because He supplies our every need! Let this be your focus today: take the Scripture that speaks the most to you today and speak it all day long.

Journal notes:

DAY 93

Stage 1: Caterpillar (remember he devours much food in preparation) First, read the Scripture to yourself.

Psalms 111 "I praise You Lord. I will praise You Lord with my whole heart among Your people, in the congregation. **2) For Your works O Lord are great and mighty and to be sought by all those who have pleasure in You.** 3) Your work is honorable and glorious. Your Righteousness endures forever. 4) You have made Your wonderful and mighty works to be remembered. You are gracious and full of compassion. 5) You give food to those who hold You in reverence. You have never forgotten Your covenant (with Your people). 6) You show Your people the power of Your mighty works. And You give us the inheritance, the goods of the heathen! (You transfer their wealth to us!) 7) The works of Your Hands are truth and justice. All Your commandments are sure (steadfast and unmovable). 8)Your commandments stand forever and ever. They are done in truth and righteousness! 9) You sent redemption unto us. You have given Your Covenant to stand forever. Holy and to be reverenced is Your Name! 10) To revere You is the beginning of being wise. To have understanding means we do Your commandments. Praise be to You forever and ever. Amen!"

Stage 2: Pupa (he goes into a state of seclusion) **Rewrite the Scripture in your own handwriting.** Then meditate a few minutes on the meaning of these wonderful scriptures. This is important to help get the Word into your heart.

Stage 3: Butterfly (Maturity comes about as you <u>let the Word work in you.</u>) **Read, pray, or sing these verses out loud two or three times to God.** When writing this down myself, I couldn't get past verse 2. Its awesomeness kept me there awhile. I said verse 2 over and over out loud. And I realized the time we are living in there will be a great manifestation of God's Power on the earth. If you think of the things God did in Moses' day, and what He is doing now in the earth; what He will do will so exceed anything God has

shown us before. His Power, Glory and Holiness will soon become an every day event! And it will be heard about every where; even the media will be showing it. God will not be out done by Satan's manifestations of power! For today, speak verse 2 all day.

Journal notes:

DAY 94

Stage 1: Caterpillar (remember he devours much food in preparation) First, read the Scripture to yourself.

Psalms 112:1-9 "I praise You Lord. For You said 'Blessed is the man (person) who fears (reveres) You deeply; and who greatly delights in Your commandments (Your Word).' 2) For that man's children shall be mighty upon the earth! My children shall be blessed! 3) Wealth and riches shall be in my house and my righteousness will endure forever! 4) Unto us (the upright in heart) there arises a light in the darkness. (God teaches me to be) gracious, full of compassion and righteous. 5) (God teaches us to) show favor, to lend, to guide our affairs with (wisdom and) discretion. 6) We will not be moved forever (for our stance is firm). We shall be remembered forever for we are in righteousness. 7) Because our heart is fixed and trusting firmly in the Lord, we shall not fear evil tidings (reports). 8) Our heart has been established by God. (That is what God is doing in you now.) Therefore we shall not be afraid. We will see our enemy perish along the way. 9) We disperse and give to the poor. Because we do, our righteousness will endure forever. Honor will be on our name."

Stage 2: Pupa (he goes into a state of seclusion) **Rewrite the Scripture in your own handwriting.** Then meditate a few minutes on the meaning of these wonderful scriptures. This is important to help get the Word into your heart.

Stage 3: Butterfly (Maturity comes about as you <u>let the Word work in you.</u>) **Read, pray, or sing these verses out loud two or three times to God.** Verse 2 is a promise to me concerning my children and grandchildren. If I will hold God in reverence in my heart and spend my time delighting myself in His Word; then my children and grandchildren will become nobles upon the earth and greatly blessed. A noble man is respected among the godly. God's Hand is upon him to bless him. That is the desire of every parent for their child. No one dreams of their child becoming a rebellious, fugitive lawbreaker who has no respect from the community. As we love the Word of God and teach

it to our children, so they will love the Word of God and they will earnestly follow after the Lord! Verse 7 says fix your heart to focus on the Lord. Set the dial on 'trusting God' and leave it there. Then when an evil report comes, you will not be in fear like the rest of the world around you. For your heart will be established; firmly positioned, unmovable. Boy, wouldn't Satan love to shake you loose from that position! But he does not have the power to move you if your mind and heart is set and firmly fixed, trusting in God! Let this be your focus today: take the Scripture that speaks the most to you today and speak it all day long.

Journal notes:

DAY 95

Stage 1: Caterpillar (remember he devours much food in preparation) First, read the Scripture to yourself.

Psalms 113 "I praise You Lord. O ye servants of the Lord, praise His Holy Name. 2) Blessed is the Name of the Lord forever. 3) From sunrise to sunset, Your Name Lord is to be praised! 4) Lord, You are high above all nations; Your Glory is above the heavens! 5) Tell me, who is like our God who dwells on high? 6) Lord, You look down and see the heavens and the earth. 7) You raise the poor up out of the dust; and (You) lift the needy out of their mess. 8) Then You set them among princes. 9) You cause the barren woman to give child; to be a joyful mother of children. I praise You Lord!"

Psalms 114:7-8 "Tremble earth at the Presence of the Lord (for He is a Holy God). Tremble at the Presence of the God of Jacob 8) for He caused water to flow from a rock!"

Stage 2: Pupa (he goes into a state of seclusion) **Rewrite the Scripture in your own handwriting.** Then meditate a few minutes on the meaning of these wonderful scriptures. This is important to help get the Word into your heart.

Stage 3: Butterfly (Maturity comes about as you let the Word work in you.) **Read, pray, or sing these verses out loud two or three times to God.** Mighty is the Lord our God! As a whole, our nation has lost its ability to praise God. Praise brings victory. Remember the fall of the walls of Jericho? (Joshua 6). It is no fairy tale. It truly happened. The thick impenetrable walls of Jericho fell when the Israelites marched around it in obedience 7 times and shouted on the 7th time! Victory came in obedience and shouts of praise! We (God's people) have kept quiet long enough! Today write your dilemma on a piece of paper. Then put it on the floor in the middle of the room. Find the Scripture God has given you concerning that matter. March around it 6 times. On the 7th time, declare that Scripture out loud over that issue 7 times and then shout with praise to God for the victory! Don't be

intimidated or concerned with 'feeling foolish' because you are marching and talking out loud. That is a tool of the devil to keep you from what God wants to give you! Declare all day that you have the victory because God is your God!

Journal notes:

DAY 96

Stage 1: Caterpillar (remember he devours much food in preparation) First, read the Scripture to yourself.

Psalms 115:1-5, 7-9, 11-16, 18 "Not unto us, O Lord; not unto us, but unto Your Name we give the glory because of Your mercy and Your truth. 2) The heathen might say 'where is your God?' 3) We tell you plainly. Our God is God of the heavens. He does as He pleases. 4) The heathen's gods are silver and gold; created by their own hands, 5) with mouths which cannot speak; eyes which cannot see, 7) and with hands and feet which are useless. 8) They created a useless god; which cannot help them in times of dilemma. 9) But Israel, trust in the Lord for He is our help and our shield of protection. 11) All who revere the Lord, place your trust in Him for He will help you and protect you. 12) He has not forgotten me. He will bless me. 13) The Lord blesses all those who revere Him in their heart. 14) The Lord will increase me more and more; me and my children. 15) I am blessed by the Lord who made heaven and earth! 16) The heavens are His; but the earth He has given to us. 18) We will praise the Lord from this time forth and forever more. Praise Your Name Lord!"

Stage 2: Pupa (he goes into a state of seclusion) **Rewrite the Scripture in your own handwriting.** Then meditate a few minutes on the meaning of these wonderful scriptures. This is important to help get the Word into your heart.

Stage 3: Butterfly (Maturity comes about as you <u>let the Word work in you.</u>) **Read, pray, or sing these verses out loud two or three times to God.** Reverence in our heart for God is a #1 priority with God. Therefore it is a matter we must give time and attention to. We cannot just train the behavior without a heart transformation. Teaching reverence begins when we are children. Look back to your childhood and see if you learned a reverential fear of God. If not, you may have to open your heart to Him now for 'heart surgery'. Either way, we can all use more reverential fear of God. It is respect for the fact that He is God, and we are not. It is a humbling of ourselves

before Him. And it is worshipping Him for who He really is - the God of the Universe. And then there is praise. We cannot truly praise without reverence for Him in our heart. He is a God of Love and mercy! He is so powerful that He spoke and all of creation began. Those are powerful reasons to praise Him! He sent His Son to be punished for our sins because of His Great Love. And He is still today reaching out to the hurting and lost because He is Great Love! He is majestic and beautiful to look upon. He is so holy we cannot even imagine! There is so much to praise Him for! His angels are all around you daily just **waiting for you to <u>give voice to God's Word concerning your situation</u>**. We must replace our grumbling with praise! Praise is faith that God is God. And God has prepared all things just for you! Praise Him today for all He is and all He does for you! Give voice all day today to the Word of God concerning your situation.

Journal notes:

DAY 97

<u>Stage 1: Caterpillar</u> (remember he devours much food in preparation) First, read the Scripture to yourself.

Psalms 116:1-2, 5-9, 12, 16-17 "I love You Lord! No matter what my problem is, You hear my need and answer. 2) You lean toward me to hear me. I will call upon Your Name as long as I live. I love You Lord! 5) You are so gracious toward me. Righteous and merciful is what You are. 6) You preserve (keep safe) the simple, humble. When I was brought low, You were my help. 7) My soul can rest, because the Lord deals bountifully with me! 8) You delivered me from death and destruction. When I cried, You wiped my tears; when I stumbled, You were there to keep my feet in the way! (Who is better to me than You!) 9) I will choose to walk in Your ways all the days of my life. 12) How could I possibly repay You Lord for all You have done for me? 16) Thank You Lord for You have freed me from the bondage of darkness! 17) I will continually praise You God and offer You the sacrifice of thanksgiving! I will call upon the Name of the Lord for You are mighty and holy. You are worthy to be praised!"

Psalms 117 "O praise the Lord, people. Praise Him for you have so much to be thankful for. 2) His mercy and goodness are great toward us. His truth will endure forever. Don't you see how good He is to us? Praise His Name. Praise His Name. Praise His Name!"

<u>Stage 2: Pupa</u> (he goes into a state of seclusion) **Rewrite the Scripture in your own handwriting.** Then meditate a few minutes on the meaning of these wonderful scriptures. This is important to help get the Word into your heart.

෨ 🦋 ෨

Stage 3: Butterfly (Maturity comes about as you <u>let the Word work in you.</u>) **Read, pray, or sing these verses out loud two or three times to God.** Let this be your focus today: take the Scripture that speaks the most to you today and speak it all day long.

Journal notes:

DAY 98

Stage 1: Caterpillar (remember he devours much food in preparation) First, read the Scripture to yourself.

Psalms 118:1-8, 10, 14-17, 19-29 "I shall give thanks unto You Lord, for You are good to me. Your mercy is extended to me forever. 2) Let us pronounce out loud together that His mercy is forever. 3) Let Israel now declare Your mercy is forever. 4) Let all who revere You say Your mercy is forever toward us. 5) When I call upon You in my distress, You answer me. You raise me above my dilemma and You set me in a large and bountiful place! 6) You are on my side therefore I will not fear. What can man do to me with You on my side? 7) You have taken my side. 8) It is better to trust in the Lord than to put my confidence in man. (Man has failing points. God has none. You will never fail or disappoint me!) 10) In the Name of the Lord I will destroy my enemies (because God is on my side!) 14) You Lord are my strength and my song. You are my salvation. 15) The sound of rejoicing is in the dwelling place of the righteous; for the Right Hand of the Lord does valiantly defend me! 16) Your Right Hand is exalted. 17) **I shall live and not die; and declare the works of the Lord!** 19) Open to me the gates of righteousness. I will go in and praise Your Name O Lord! 20) The righteous shall enter into the gate of the Lord! 21) I will praise You for You have heard my cry and saved me! 22) The stone which the builders rejected is become the corner stone. 23) This is the Lord's doing; and it is marvelous in our eyes. 24) This is the day that the Lord has made. I will rejoice and be glad in today! 25) Send now prosperity, Lord. 26) Blessed is he who comes in the Name of the Lord. You are blessed out of the dwelling place of the Lord! 27) God is the Lord. Lord, You have shown us light. 28) You are my God! And I will forever praise You! You are my God and I exalt Your Holy Name! 29) O I praise You and thank You God for You are so good to me. Your mercy toward me never ends!"

Stage 2: Pupa (he goes into a state of seclusion) **Rewrite the Scripture in your own handwriting.** Then meditate a few minutes on the meaning of these wonderful scriptures. This is important to help get the Word into your heart.

Stage 3: Butterfly (Maturity comes about as you <u>let the Word work in you.</u>)
Read, pray, or sing these verses out loud two or three times to God.
Wow! What an amazing chapter! There are so many marvelous promises in this chapter. There are so many good things to declare out loud daily. The best declaration to me is verse 28: You are my God! Other declarations: Vs. 15 The sound of rejoicing is in the dwelling place of the righteous; for the Lord's Hand defends me! Vs. 17 I shall live and not die; and I shall declare the works of the Lord! Vs 24 This is the day that the Lord has made. I will rejoice and be glad in it! Vs 25 Thank You Lord that You send NOW prosperity! Vs 29: Your mercy toward me never ends! Let this be your focus today: take the Scripture that speaks the most to you today and speak it all day long.

Journal notes:

DAY 99

Stage 1: Caterpillar (remember he devours much food in preparation) First, read the Scripture to yourself.

Psalms 119:1-8 ALEPH "Blessed are the undefiled in the Lord's way; those who (really) walk in obedience to the Lord. 2) Blessed are they who keep the Word of the Lord; who seek God with their whole heart! 3) They also do not engage in iniquity; they walk in the Lord's ways. 4) For You O Lord have commanded us to be diligent in keeping Your commandments. 5) Direct my ways O Lord that I may keep Your laws! 6) Thus I will never be shame-faced for I respect Your commandments. 7) I shall praise You God with an upright heart for You teach me Your righteous judgments. 8) I declare I will keep Your statutes."

Stage 2: Pupa (he goes into a state of seclusion) **Rewrite the Scripture in your own handwriting.** Then meditate a few minutes on the meaning of these wonderful scriptures. This is important to help get the Word into your heart.

Stage 3: Butterfly (Maturity comes about as you let the Word work in you.) **Read, pray, or sing these verses out loud two or three times to God.** Blessed are they who keep the Word of the Lord and seek God with their whole heart! Wholeheartedly run after God. Lord, You are beautiful, magnificent, Holy, glorious and mighty! I Love You! Let this be your focus today: take the Scripture that speaks the most to you today and speak it all day long.

Journal notes:

DAY 100

<u>Stage 1: Caterpillar</u> (remember he devours much food in preparation) First, read the Scripture to yourself.

Psalms 119:9-16 BETH "How does one be cleansed? By taking heed to Your Word, O Lord. 10) Lord, with my whole heart I have sought You, I do seek You. Let me never wander from You or Your laws. 11) Your Word is securely hid in my heart to keep me from sinning against You. 12) I praise and bless Your Holy Name O Lord for You teach me Your statutes. (You redirect my heart to do right. You correct and teach me Your ways!) 13) With my mouth I will declare and do decree all the promises in Your Words. 14) I rejoice exceedingly in Your ways and Your righteous commands; more than in all the riches. (For You are joy unspeakable!) 15) I choose to meditate continually on Your Word and I cause my heart to respect/ to revere You and Your ways O holy Father. 16) I will find my greatest delights in Your Word. I will not forget Your Word; nor let it slip out of my heart! (Your Word is life to me. I must feed on it every day!)"

<u>Stage 2: Pupa</u> (he goes into a state of seclusion) **Rewrite the Scripture in your own handwriting.** Then meditate a few minutes on the meaning of these wonderful scriptures. This is important to help get the Word into your heart.

<u>Stage 3: Butterfly</u> (Maturity comes about as you <u>let the Word work in you.</u>) **Read, pray, or sing these verses out loud two or three times to God.** According to verse 12 it is the Word of God that teaches us how to live our daily life. His Spirit within us (as born again believers) takes the Word we read and pricks our heart causing it to open up and receive truth. We then take that truth we learned and think differently (this is mind renewal). The Holy Spirit gives us the power to live that truth daily (this is behavior change). We have no knowledge unless we read His Word. We have no power/ability to change ourselves without His Holy Spirit dwelling in us (this happens when we are born again). So God has given us all we need; we have no excuse. Verses

10-16 talks of our heart desiring God above all else and making His Word a priority in our life! Let this be your focus today: take the Scripture that speaks the most to you today and speak it all day long.

Journal notes:

DAY 101

Stage 1: Caterpillar (remember he devours much food in preparation) First, read the Scripture to yourself.

Psalms 119:17-24 GIMEL "You deal bountifully with me; that I may live and keep Your Word. 18) You open my sight that I may see the truth in Your Word. 19) Although I am a foreigner in the earth; You have revealed Your commandments to me. 20) My heart and soul deeply long for Your Words. 21) You rebuke the proud for they err from Your commandments (into their own way. But You keep me on the right path.) 22) You remove reproach, contempt and shame from my name as I keep Your testimonies. 23) You have taught me to keep my mind on Your Word. Even when I am lied about, I keep my mind on Your Word. 24) For Your Word is my utmost delight. It guides me, and counsels me in all affairs of life!"

Stage 2: Pupa (he goes into a state of seclusion) So you will **rewrite the Scripture in your own handwriting.** Then meditate a few minutes on the meaning of these wonderful scriptures. This is important to help get the Word into your heart.

Stage 3: Butterfly (Maturity comes about as you let the Word work in you.) **Read, pray, or sing these verses out loud two or three times to God.** In verse 23, we see that keeping our mind on the Word is of the utmost importance when we are under any kind of attack from the devil. To keep our mind on the Word in difficult times, we must love the Word of God and hunger for it; always keeping our time in the Word like an important appointment. All 8 verses today deal with the Word of God. His written Word- the Bible- is just as if He came today and spoke it to you. Every verse above tells us we must read the Word. We must think about the Word - in fact we must keep it foremost in our minds. We must love the Word. And we must obey the Word. In Joshua 1:7 God told Joshua (among other things) not to turn from the Word to the left nor to the right. It is sometimes so easy to just make a slight compromise in our daily living. But even a slight turn takes us off of the right (straight) path and out into the jungle where we become prey for dangerous situations. God warns us not to compromise, but to stick on the straight path of His Word. It is vital for our lives these days! Let this be your focus today: take the Scripture that speaks the most to you today and speak it all day long.

Journal notes:

DAY 102

Stage 1: Caterpillar (remember he devours much food in preparation) First, read the Scripture to yourself.

Psalms 119:25-32 DALETH "When my soul nears death; Lord, You revive me with Your Word. 26) I declare with my mouth and You hear; You teach me right from wrong. 27) You give me understanding in your Ways. I shall continually praise Your wondrous and mighty works! **(Every day I see the beauty of Your Power in all of creation. And because of it I know You are a mighty and a good God! Your Love and Mercy are poured out on us every day! I pray our eyes be opened that we may recognize how magnificent You are and worship You for it!)** 28) When my soul melts under the heaviness of life, You strengthen me with Your Word! 29) You remove from me a lying tongue and grant to me Your law graciously. 30) I shall choose the truth. I will keep Your Law before my eyes (and in my heart). 31) I will stick (like glue) to Your Words, O Lord; thus I will not be ashamed. 32) I will run to Your Ways and Your commandments, for <u>You O God increase love, joy and peace in my heart.</u>"

Stage 2: Pupa (he goes into a state of seclusion) So you will **rewrite the Scripture in your own handwriting.** Then meditate a few minutes on the meaning of these wonderful scriptures. This is important to help get the Word into your heart.

Stage 3: Butterfly (Maturity comes about as you <u>let the Word work in you.</u>) **Read, pray, or sing these verses out loud two or three times to God.** So much anger and hurt has broken off of me during these 150 days of praise. As I focus each day on God's goodness, old and new hurts alike are healed by His Love. **His Love is greater than any wound of our soul. But it can only come in and heal us as we give God access to our heart.** Focusing every day on His magnificence helps us do just that! A peace-filled life is one that forgives all wrongs done to us right away; holding no grudges. I am learning to do that. My joy and quality of life are improving daily. As my joy improves, so does my health! God also promises in verse 27 that He will give us understanding. We must visit with Him a lot in quiet time to get understanding. How do you think all the great scientists made 'their' discoveries? They spent time with God and He gave them understanding and wisdom. He will also do it for us. God wants our thinking and understanding to expand. He wants to 'walk and talk with us in the garden' as He did with Adam and Eve. God loves one-on-one with us. Sometimes I just look out at nature and tell Him over and over how much I love Him. When I do, He fills my heart with peace and joy. Only God could imagine and create green leaves, grass, 1000 types of flowers, all of the animal kingdom, and the complex human body. Only God could create a human soul which will never cease to exist. We are the most unique and marvelous of His creations. Once death comes to other creations, they no longer exist. But once created, humans will exist forever either in heaven or hell. That is some creativeness. He is more powerful than we can even imagine at this point. We are created and yet the Creator wants to teach us to create a little like He does. He wants to work 'hand-in-hand' with us, making new and exciting things for the world like He and Thomas Edison did. God wants to work in us and through us in so many ways; like our words. We can change things around us by speaking the Word of God out loud over situations. When we speak in faith what God says over a problem, it is as if God Himself were talking to that situation; and things change! As we open our hearts and minds to God we can experience good lives today! Let this be your focus today: take the Scripture that speaks the most to you today and speak it all day long.

Journal notes:

DAY 103

Stage 1: Caterpillar (remember he devours much food in preparation) First, read the Scripture to yourself.

Psalms 119:33-40 HE "You have taught me Your way O Lord; and You strengthen me to keep it to the end. 34) You have given me understanding to keep Your laws. You help me to observe it with my whole heart. 35) You cause me to walk upright in Your Word and Your commandments. **I delight to do Your Will.** 36) You incline my heart unto Your Word and You draw me away from the things of the world. 37) You turn my heart away from wickedness and unto You. You have revived me in Your Ways. 38) Lord, establish Your Word in me as You teach me reverential fear. 39) You have turned away my reproach. (My shameful past is gone and remembered no more! It is not accounted to me in any way!) Your justice is so good toward me! 40) I love and long for Your Word to fill me. Your Righteousness makes me alive again!"

Stage 2: Pupa (he goes into a state of seclusion) So you will **rewrite the Scripture in your own handwriting.** Then meditate a few minutes on the meaning of these wonderful scriptures. This is important to help get the Word into your heart.

Stage 3: Butterfly (Maturity comes about as you <u>let the Word work in you.</u>) **Read, pray, or sing these verses out loud two or three times to God.** As if we don't have enough to thank God for in that: 1) He gave us life; and 2) He forgives all our sins. Then God tops it all off with renewing our dignity by wiping out even the memory and shame of our pasts. He doesn't remember them. He helps us forget. And He even restores us to a place of respect in our communities and family; clearly washing out our past forever. God is so much more faithful than we'll ever know or be able to thank Him for. He is a repairer of the breaches in our lives, our soul and our relationships with others! The way to this victory is outlined in verses 33-38. Read them again. They all talk of God's Word being put in our heart; and our heart choosing God's Word over anything this world can offer. That is the key to all of life's successes. Look at the famous men in the bible: Moses, Abraham, Joshua and

King David. They all whole-heartedly chose God. Even when they fell, they repented; because it broke their heart that they failed their God. God is not interested in finding perfect people - there are none. He is looking for men and women whose hearts desire Him; people who love Him above all. This segment of verses 33-40 also shows it is our will, but it is God's Power that enables our willingness. Verse 33 says God strengthens us. Verse 34 says He helps us observe (keep) His laws. Verse 35 says He causes us to walk upright. Verse 36 says He inclines our heart toward His Word. Verse 37 says He turns our heart from wickedness. Verse 38 says He establishes His Word in us as He teaches us reverential fear. (This verse 38 is my personal favorite in this segment of verses.) This all shows we have no power against sin without God. But we as humans have a will. We can choose who our heart is devoted to. Satan wants us to choose him, so he can kill us. God wants us to choose Him so He can give us victory and a good life now; plus eternal life in a place of love and many wonders. If we choose God, we must choose His Word and verse 38 says He will establish it in our heart (as we study the Word)! Let this be your focus today: take the Scripture that speaks the most to you today and speak it all day long.

Journal notes:

DAY 104

Stage 1: Caterpillar (remember he devours much food in preparation) First, read the Scripture to yourself.

Psalms 119:41-48 VAU "Thank You Lord that Your mercies are given to me and Your salvation is in Your Word. 42) This will be my answer to him who mocks me; for I place my trust in Your Word! 43) Thank You that You do not take the Word of truth out of my mouth; for my hope is in Your Righteous justice! 44) This is the way I shall keep Your law continually; even forever and ever. 45) You teach me to walk in freedom because I seek your precepts. 46) You teach me to speak of Your testimonies even before highest rulers and not be ashamed of it. (I am not afraid to declare Your Word.) 47) You teach me to put my delight in Your commandments, to dearly love Your way. 48) I praise You for Your commandments, for I love them and I will meditate in them day and night."

Stage 2: Pupa (he goes into a state of seclusion) So you will **rewrite the Scripture in your own handwriting.** Then meditate a few minutes on the meaning of these wonderful scriptures. This is important to help get the Word into your heart.

Stage 3: Butterfly (Maturity comes about as you <u>let the Word work in you.</u>) **Read, pray, or sing these verses out loud two or three times to God.** I recently learned that to meditate means 'to mutter or speak it out loud continually'! Of course, you must think something in order to speak it. But for meditation to actually mean to speak out loud continually, changes what I always thought. I thought it just meant to think. But it means so much more than just to think. **We are to speak the Word of God continually.** And as we do, faith arises. Circumstances change to the Glory of God! Verse 41 says salvation and mercy are in His Word. Verse 47 says we should delight and love His Word. Since salvation and mercy are in His Word, then we should love His Word! Verse 43 says when His Word is in our mouth, truth is in our mouth. Verse 44 shows that **keeping the Word in our mouth (and mind and heart) is what keeps us on the right path!** Keeping His Word in our

mouth continually keeps us free from things that bind those who do not keep the Word (verse 45). Keeping His Word in our mouth even before our highest authority is important and we are not to be ashamed of it (verse 46). His Word must be our delight. And we must speak it out continually. That puts it in our mind (to change our thinking); in our heart (to change our behavior); and in our mouth (to glorify God, and to change our circumstances)! Let this be your focus today: take the Scripture that speaks the most to you today and speak it all day long.

Journal notes:

DAY 105

Stage 1: Caterpillar (remember he devours much food in preparation) First, read the Scripture to yourself.

Psalms 119:49-56 ZAIN "You remind me of Your Word; in which You have caused me to have hope. 50) And when I am distressed and in trouble, Your Word brings life to me once again. 51) Although the wicked may come against me, I will not leave Your laws. 52) <u>Your Word comforts me</u>, and I remember that You have always given justice. 53) I see the wicked have forsaken Your Ways. 54) But I will sing of Your Grace, Your Mercy and Your Truth forever. 55) You cause me to remember the Holiness of Your Name day and night. You teach me to keep Your law. 56) In everything, You teach me to keep Your precepts!"

Stage 2: Pupa (he goes into a state of seclusion) So you will **rewrite the Scripture in your own handwriting.** Then meditate a few minutes on the meaning of these wonderful scriptures. This is important to help get the Word into your heart.

Stage 3: Butterfly (Maturity comes about as you <u>let the Word work in you.</u>) **Read, pray, or sing these verses out loud two or three times to God.** In the Old Testament times, there was a better understanding of the Holiness of God's Name. His Name was so sacred to them, they wouldn't even speak it. We have lost a great deal of reverence for God in our days. It must be renewed. He is to be praised if for no other reason, just for His Holiness. Yet there are so many other reasons to praise Him! For His amazing, unending mercy on us (we do not seem to realize the depth of His mercy)! Verse 49 says in His Word is where hope begins. He reminds us to keep his Word close in our hearts. Verse 50 says His Word brings life. Verse 52 says His Word gives comfort and reminds us that God will always give justice. In short His Word is Him. In putting the Word of God in our heart, we are inviting God in there. In inviting God in, we are able to have hope with life continually flowing in, refreshing and revitalizing us. We are given mercy, joy and justice (when our enemy comes against us)! How dumb not to receive all these blessings of the Lord! Being born again, we have His Word AND His Spirit within us! That gives us all we need to live a good and a victorious life! Let this be your focus today: take the Scripture that speaks the most to you today and speak it all day long.

Journal notes:

DAY 106

Stage 1: Caterpillar (remember he devours much food in preparation) First, read the Scripture to yourself.

Psalms 119:57-64 CHETH "<u>You are my portion O Lord!</u> I declare that I will keep Your Words. 58) I seek Your favor with my whole heart. I know You will be merciful to me according to Your Word. 59) I thought on my ways and turned my feet to Your commandments. 60) I shall be happy to make haste and not delay in keeping Your commandments. 61) Although the wicked may rob me, yet I will not forget Your Ways. 62) <u>At all hours through the night, when I awake, praise and thanksgiving will be on my lips to You because You are a Righteous Judge!</u> 63) I keep company with those in reverence to You. 64) The earth O Lord is full of Your Mercy; teach me Your Ways O Lord!"

Stage 2: Pupa (he goes into a state of seclusion) So you will **rewrite the Scripture in your own handwriting.** Then meditate a few minutes on the meaning of these wonderful scriptures. This is important to help get the Word into your heart.

Stage 3: Butterfly (Maturity comes about as you <u>let the Word work in you.</u>) **Read, pray, or sing these verses out loud two or three times to God.** I'm so grateful God is my portion (verse 57). Imagine someone is handing out inheritance gifts. When they come to you, instead of leaving you money, houses or cars, your lot (of inheritance) is to have God forever on your side! That is what verse 57 says to me. He is my portion! I would rather have God as my inheritance than anything in this world. Years ago when my father passed away, I gave his eulogy. Part of what I said was that our father didn't leave my brothers and me money, or a lot of material possessions. What he did leave us was much better. It was a teaching in the Lord. Our parents taught us growing up that our relationship with God was the most important thing. That was the finest inheritance they could leave us. There is no greater gift we can give to our children than leading them to have a deep relationship with God through Jesus and the Word of God. God is my portion and I am so grateful for my inheritance from my parents - the fact that they taught me about God and thus led me to Him! We should give thanks to God at all times. Let this be your focus today: take the Scripture that speaks the most to you today and speak it all day long.

Journal notes:

DAY 107

Stage 1: Caterpillar (remember he devours much food in preparation) First, read the Scripture to yourself.

Psalms 119:65-72 TETH "Thank You Lord, for You have been so very good to me according to Your Word. 66) You teach me good judgment and knowledge because I believe your commandments. 67) I am sorry that I turned away from You. My sin brought affliction; but now I keep your Word. 68) You are so good and You do good. Teach me Your Ways O Lord. 69) Although I am lied about, yet I will keep your laws with my whole heart. 70) The sinner's heart is full of sin; but my whole delight is in You Lord. 71) It was in my affliction that I learned Your statutes. 72) Your Words now are better to me than all the gold and silver in the world!"

Stage 2: Pupa (he goes into a state of seclusion) So you will **rewrite the Scripture in your own handwriting.** Then meditate a few minutes on the meaning of these wonderful scriptures. This is important to help get the Word into your heart.

Stage 3: Butterfly (Maturity comes about as you <u>let the Word work in you.</u>) **Read, pray, or sing these verses out loud two or three times to God.** Will we ever know the depths of the goodness of God toward us? Your Word O God reaches into the depths of my soul and shines a light on the darkness, exposing and evicting it! The light then begins to spread to all parts of my heart, chasing out all the old wounds and unforgiveness. The hardened parts soften once again in the glow of Your Love. Hope is revived like a flower in the spring. It gives beauty once again to my life! I have been without hope before. To have hope is better! Let this be your focus today: take the Scripture that speaks the most to you today and speak it all day long.

Journal notes:

DAY 108

Stage 1: Caterpillar (remember he devours much food in preparation) First, read the Scripture to yourself.

Psalms 119:73-80 JOD "Your Hands have made me and fashioned me. You give me understanding so I may learn Your commandments. (I adore You, Father.) 74) I put my hope in Your Word. 75) I know, Lord, that Your judgments are righteous and that <u>You in faithfulness have corrected me</u>. 76) So <u>I ask that Your merciful kindness be given me, to comfort me, just as Your Word promises to do!</u> 77) That Your tender mercies will come to me that I may live; for Your law is what I delight in! 78) The proud will be ashamed for they dealt unjustly with me without a cause. Yet I will meditate in Your precepts. (Your Word is life to me and I will keep my mind on it.) 79) Those who love You will turn again to me and those who know Your Word. 80) May my heart be sound, solid as a rock, stable, unmovable in Your statutes of what is right. And I will not be put to shame (because I will not move off of what is right)!"

Stage 2: Pupa (he goes into a state of seclusion) So you will **rewrite the Scripture in your own handwriting.** Then meditate a few minutes on the meaning of these wonderful scriptures. This is important to help get the Word into your heart.

Stage 3: Butterfly (Maturity comes about as you <u>let the Word work in you.</u>) **Read, pray, or sing these verses out loud two or three times to God.** Even in times when God must correct us, He still gives us His mercy! Correction with mercy shows us we are not rejected just because we have made mistakes! That is good news to me! Let this be your focus today: take the Scripture that speaks the most to you today and speak it all day long.

Journal notes:

DAY 109

Stage 1: Caterpillar (remember he devours much food in preparation) First, read the Scripture to yourself.

Psalms 119:81-88 CAPH "My soul longs for Your salvation, Lord. I put my hope in Your Word. 82) My eyes diligently keep watch for You to come and comfort me! I desire it greatly. 83) Although I become old, yet I shall never forget Your statutes. (I will never leave You for You are my God.) 84) I may not know how long my life will be. But I do know You will execute judgment on my enemies. 85) They break Your laws and set traps for me. 86) But I know Your commandments are sure and steadfast. **Faithful is Your Name. You are my help.** 87) Although my enemy almost overtook me, I would not forsake Your Ways. 88) Revive my life according to your loving kindness O Lord. I shall keep the testimony (Word) that comes forth from Your Mouth!"

Stage 2: Pupa (he goes into a state of seclusion) So you will **rewrite the Scripture in your own handwriting.** Then meditate a few minutes on the meaning of these wonderful scriptures. This is important to help get the Word into your heart.

Stage 3: Butterfly (Maturity comes about as you <u>let the Word work in you.</u>) **Read, pray, or sing these verses out loud two or three times to God.** God is so very faithful to me. I learn that every day for He always brings me through my dilemmas - big or small. He is faithful even if we are not. But when we keep His commandments it opens many doors of blessings for us. Keeping His commandments means first and foremost love and obey God above all other things/people in your life. Love Him because He is God and He is faithful. Our heart toward Him changes when we decide to love Him. When our heart is open to Him, all things are possible. Praise helps open our heart to Him. Reverence for Him keeps it open! Let this be your focus today: take the Scripture that speaks the most to you today and speak it all day long.

Journal notes:

DAY 110

Stage 1: Caterpillar (remember he devours much food in preparation) First, read the Scripture to yourself.

Psalms 119:89-96 LAMED "**Forever, O Lord, Your Word is settled in heaven!** 90) Your faithfulness is to all generations. For You have established the earth and it abides forever. 91) All creation is still in existence today (sun, moon, stars, earth, etc) because You commanded it to be so. They must obey You. 92) I would have perished in my affliction long ago had it not been that my delight was in Your laws! 93) I shall never forget Your precepts; for with them you have revived me. 94) I am Yours; and You save me for I seek Your Ways. 95) Although the wicked seek to destroy me, yet I will keep to Your Word. 96) There has been an end to some things. **But Your Word never ends, nor ceases to exist, nor fails to save me!**"

Stage 2: Pupa (he goes into a state of seclusion) So you will **rewrite the Scripture in your own handwriting.** Then meditate a few minutes on the meaning of these wonderful scriptures. This is important to help get the Word into your heart.

Stage 3: Butterfly (Maturity comes about as you <u>let the Word work in you.</u>) **Read, pray, or sing these verses out loud two or three times to God.** All of these verses declare that God's Word is forever. It will never be obsolete or cease to exist or fail to save us! What better comfort is there than this? God's faithfulness never ends. When God speaks, that Word stands and remains forever! When God says something is so, it is! Nothing can change it or cause His Word to fail! Stand on that today knowing nothing can stop what God has promised you from coming to pass! **God is faithful!**

Journal notes:

DAY 111

Stage 1: Caterpillar (remember he devours much food in preparation) First, read the Scripture to yourself.

Psalms 119:97-104 MEM "**O how I love Your Word O Lord. It is continually in my mind, my heart and my mouth all day long!** 98) Through Your Word, You have made me wiser than my enemies. I cannot go a day without Your Word for my enemies are always near. 99) You have given me more understanding than my teachers (and elders) because my mind and mouth are continually on Your Word. 100) I understand more than the people before me, because I keep Your commandments. 101) Keeping Your Word causes me to keep my feet from going the way of evil. 102) I will not depart from Your judgments. You are my teacher! 103) I adore You. I adore Your Word. It is as sweet to me as honey in my mouth. (It puts joy in my heart!) 104) In Your Word I receive understanding. I see plainly the way of wickedness and I hate it. I will not go that path!"

Stage 2: Pupa (he goes into a state of seclusion) So you will **rewrite the Scripture in your own handwriting.** Then meditate a few minutes on the meaning of these wonderful scriptures. This is important to help get the Word into your heart.

Stage 3: Butterfly (Maturity comes about as you <u>let the Word work in you.</u>) **Read, pray, or sing these verses out loud two or three times to God.** I am hooked on God's Word. I cannot go a day without it! There is such joy in His Word. Lord, You put joy and hope in my soul! Real success in this life is falling in love with God, Jesus and the Holy Spirit. God will make all you do to prosper quite easily once your total focus is on Him. He will elevate you above your peers because your heart will be established on loving Him above all people and things. (To establish is to secure and set in concrete and become unmovable!) I understand shallowness. I brought home some plants the other day and gave away most of the soil. When I re-potted the plant, I realized I did not have enough soil left to securely hold the plant upright. It kept leaning over and quickly began to wilt in the summer heat. I knew there

was not enough soil for the roots to secure and the plant would not make it in that pot. So for the plant to live, I had to plant it in the ground. Being a shallow Christian who barely spends time with our God is like that plant in a pot with not enough soil to sustain it. You will wilt and die without the proper stability in your life. You need to be anchored to something stronger than you are in order to make it through life's storms. If you know a person who has become bitter by life's experiences, then you see the sad result of not **being anchored in the love of God**. Verse 97 shows us that anchoring comes only in spending time in God's Word and His Presence. We then flourish (grow strong, lush and beautiful) with a good life. But only by falling in love with Christ, with God, with the Holy Spirit (our helper and comforter) can you make it in this life! Let becoming anchored in the Love of God become your focus today.

Journal notes:

DAY 112

Stage 1: Caterpillar (remember he devours much food in preparation) First, read the Scripture to yourself.

Psalms 119:105-112 NUN <u>"Your Word is a lamp unto my feet, and a light unto my path.</u> 106) I have sworn (declared) an oath and I will keep it. The oath (promise/declaration) is this, that I will keep Your Righteous Judgments. 107) Oh Lord, when I am afflicted, I know You will revive me according to Your Word. 108) Lord, accept the freewill offering, the praise of my mouth that comes from my heart to You. Teach me Your judgments (and justice)! 109) I will not forget Your laws though my life be at stake. 110) Although the wicked lay a trap for me, yet I will not depart from Your laws and Your Ways! 111) Your Word have I taken as an inheritance FOREVER. Your Word brings joy and rejoicing to my heart. 112) I have directed my heart to obey Your statutes always and never to end!"

Stage 2: Pupa (he goes into a state of seclusion) So you will **rewrite the Scripture in your own handwriting.** Then meditate a few minutes on the meaning of these wonderful scriptures. This is important to help get the Word into your heart.

Stage 3: Butterfly (Maturity comes about as you <u>let the Word work in you.</u>) **Read, pray, or sing these verses out loud two or three times to God.** If we ever wonder about a decision in our life, or a behavioral response to evil, we must look to the Word of God for our answer. For He said to us (in verse 105) that His Word is given to us as a lamp for our feet to know which path to take; and a light along that path (so we do not lose our way). God is saying **we are never without direction from Him**, because His Word is ever with us to direct us in everything we need in this life. Our part is to put His Word in our heart and keep it there. Trust God today for direction by quoting verse 105 aloud every time you must make a decision.

Journal notes:

DAY 113

Stage 1: Caterpillar (remember he devours much food in preparation) First, read the Scripture to yourself.

Psalms 119:113-120 SAMECH "**I hate wasteful thoughts; but Your Word I do love (to meditate on).** 114) **You are my hiding place and my shield.** I (put my) hope in Your Word. 115) Evildoers, depart from me; for I have determined that I will keep the commandments of my God. 116) Lord, You uphold me according to Your Word that I may live. You do not let me be ashamed of placing my hope in You (for You have never let me down). 117) You, my God hold me up so that I am safe. I will have respect for Your statutes forever. 118) You have trampled down all those who hate Your Word. 119) You put away all the wicked of the earth. Therefore I love Your Word to me. 120) I revere You Oh God. I do not want to be as the wicked on Judgment Day!"

Stage 2: Pupa (he goes into a state of seclusion) So you will **rewrite the Scripture in your own handwriting.** Then meditate a few minutes on the meaning of these wonderful scriptures. This is important to help get the Word into your heart.

Stage 3: Butterfly (Maturity comes about as you <u>let the Word work in you.</u>) **Read, pray, or sing these verses out loud two or three times to God.** Verse 114 speaks of a covering of protection by God; a safe haven in Him! There are so many songs written about running to our safe place in God! When we have a dilemma; or our feelings have been hurt, we can run to our shelter in Him; and He will make it alright! Love, money, fortune and fame, sex or drugs - none of these can relieve our emptiness or heal our hurts. But God can heal anything and everything. Verse 117 says again that He will keep us safe. Verses 113 and 114 show that there is a connection between keeping our mind on His Word and Him keeping us in the safe hiding place. One example of that to me is when tormenting thoughts come. We are to put God's Word in our mind and kick out those tormenting thoughts. Torment in our mind is a big tool of the devil (our enemy). When we allow those thoughts to remain, our heart begins to fear, hurt and break. Mental torment is a horrible place to be.

What we think during the day matters! But we do not have to remain there. Get out the Word of God. Put it in your mind. Kick out those thoughts from the devil that are hurting you. **Open your mouth and speak the Word of God until the tormenting thoughts have to leave!** (I shouted that part to you because you must understand how important that part is.) When you kick out the tormenting thoughts and do not believe them, **this is you choosing God's Word over the enemy's**. Choose to put God's Word in your mind. **Meditating on the Word of God moves us into His hiding place with a shield around us.** We can choose to be in God's hiding place; or we can let wasteful and vain thoughts fill our mind tormenting us. God can shield us from the things that hurt us and from the people who hate Him, if we will let Him. We can love God, and yet be emotionally beat up if we do not know how to **get into His hiding place**. This is done by **keeping His Word in our mind and coming out of our mouth.** At work when something troubles me, I mutter to myself the Scripture God brings to my mind. I do not care what people think. I remain sane and full of joy by talking to myself many times; filling my heart with the Word and remaining behind God's shield. Many an opportunity to get my feelings hurt has been passed over when I remain behind His shield! Let this be your focus today: take the Scripture that speaks the most to you today and speak it all day long.

Journal notes:

DAY 114

Stage 1: Caterpillar (remember he devours much food in preparation) First, read the Scripture to yourself.

Psalms 119:121-128 AIN "I know You will not leave me to my oppressors, for I have done justly and have caused justice to be done. 122) I know You will be a surety for me to the good; and You will not let the proud oppress me. 123) My eyes long to see Your salvation; and they long for the Word of Your righteousness. 124) You deal with me according to Your great mercy; and You teach me Your statutes. 125) I declare that I am Your servant. You give me understanding that I may know Your Word. 126) It is time for You to work (on my behalf, Lord). The wicked make void Your law. They ignore what is right. 127) Yet I love Your commandments above all the gold in the world! 128) I esteem (hold in the highest regard in my heart) Your Words for they are all truth and justice. And I hate every lying way. (I will keep myself from lying and false ways; for I hold Your Word in highest regard)."

Stage 2: Pupa (he goes into a state of seclusion) So you will **rewrite the Scripture in your own handwriting.** Then meditate a few minutes on the meaning of these wonderful scriptures. This is important to help get the Word into your heart.

Stage 3: Butterfly (Maturity comes about as you <u>let the Word work in you.</u>) **Read, pray, or sing these verses out loud two or three times to God.** "There is a path that <u>seems</u> right unto a man. But the end is death." (Proverbs 14:12) The right way is by staying in God's Word. His Word brings life. But as Proverbs 14:12 tells us, there is another path that those who lack understanding take; and it brings them to destruction. All understanding is in the Word of God. It is readily available to guide us in every day affairs of life. We must love it and spend time in it. Let this be your focus today: take the Scripture that speaks the most to you today and speak it all day long.

Journal notes:

DAY 115

Stage 1: Caterpillar (remember he devours much food in preparation) First, read the Scripture to yourself.

Psalms 119:129-136 PE "Your testimonies are wonderful. That is why my soul keeps them. 130) <u>The entrance of your Word gives light to my heart, mind and soul.</u> Your Word gives understanding even to the simple. 131) I longed for Your commandments. 132) I know You will look upon me and be merciful to me; as You always do to those who love Your Name. 133) Lord, order (direct) my steps in Your Word, and let no sin have dominion over me. 134) I know You will deliver me from the oppression of man, so that I can keep Your laws. 135) You make Your face to shine upon me in favor and blessings. You teach me Your statutes. 136) It makes me so sad to see others do not care to keep Your law. (Yet I love You, Lord!)"

Stage 2: Pupa (he goes into a state of seclusion) So you will **rewrite the Scripture in your own handwriting.** Then meditate a few minutes on the meaning of these wonderful scriptures. This is important to help get the Word into your heart.

Stage 3: Butterfly (Maturity comes about as you <u>let the Word work in you.</u>) **Read, pray, or sing these verses out loud two or three times to God.** You know, one of the many wonders about our God is that we do not have to beg Him to be merciful to us, to love us, to provide for us, to protect us, to heal us, to redeem and restore us! He <u>is</u> those things. He is mercy, love, provision, safety, sanctuary, healer, redeemer and restorer. People who do not intimately know Him do not know that about Him. They think they have to be perfect and beg God to move in their lives. All we have to do is spend time with Him! Then <u>we open up</u> to Him! When we open up, God has more freedom to move in our lives and on our behalf. He is eager to do for us. It is our doubting and unbelieving hearts that stop Him! God is so good to us! Praise builds our faith to believe for what He promises in His Word because the more we believe He is good, the less doubt, fear and unbelief we have! Imagine a life without fear! When your soul is FULL of PRAISE TO GOD; LOVE FOR GOD AND

TRUST IN GOD: then fear has no place left to dwell in you. Your past is forgiven and forgotten. Your present is joyous. And your future-ah, it is as bright as the new morning sun. For God is in you; and He is with you! And you and I can have that! It is not just for the super Christian. (Incidentally there is no such thing as a super-Christian!) It is for anyone who will spend the time to gain intimacy with God! Let this be your focus today: take the Scripture that speaks the most to you today and speak it all day long.

Journal notes:

DAY 116

Stage 1: Caterpillar (remember he devours much food in preparation) First, read the Scripture to yourself.

Psalms 119:137-144 TZADDI "**Lord, You are righteous**; upright are Your judgments. 138) The testimonies You have commanded (for us) are righteous **and very faithful.** (God, You are so very good to us. We can never repay You for all Your goodness!) 139) Zeal for You consumes me when I see the wicked forsaking Your Word. 140) Your Word Oh Lord, is very pure; it is holy. I love Your Word. 141) I am a nobody; but I do not forget Your laws. 142) Your Righteousness is an everlasting righteousness. Your law is the truth. 143) Even when trouble and grief take hold of me; yet my delight is in Your commandments. 144) The righteousness of Your testimony (Word) is everlasting (never-ending). When You give me understanding, I shall live!"

Stage 2: Pupa (he goes into a state of seclusion) So you will **rewrite the Scripture in your own handwriting.** Then meditate a few minutes on the meaning of these wonderful scriptures. This is important to help get the Word into your heart.

Stage 3: Butterfly (Maturity comes about as you let the Word work in you.) **Read, pray, or sing these verses out loud two or three times to God.** Joy is in loving God and knowing **He is righteous and faithful to you.** When love for God and joy bubbles up inside you, your circumstances just don't matter because you have something greater than your circumstances. It is God! Your love for Him matches your faith in Him. The more you give yourself to love Him, the greater your faith is in Him to provide for you, to answer your prayers, to heal you and restore your family. It isn't that He is waiting on you to behave better before He answers your prayer. It is that your faith must arise and take hold of what He has already given you. And your faith level rises with each rising degree of your loving Him because it opens your heart - not His. His heart is already open. He doesn't have to be begged for things. He is

a good and giving God. He is Righteous and Just. But He is also Mercy and Compassion! Praise Him today for who He is! Today declare the bold part of verses 137-138 all day long.

Journal notes:

DAY 117

<u>Stage 1: Caterpillar</u> (remember he devours much food in preparation) First, read the Scripture to yourself.

Psalms 119:145-152 KOPH "I cried with my whole heart. Hear me, Oh Lord, for I will keep Your statutes. 146) I cry out unto You God to save me so I can keep Your testimonies. 147) All night I cried and I put my hope in Your Word. 148) I was awake all night, so that I could meditate on Your Word, Lord. (This clearly shows us how important it is to spend time putting God's Word in our mind and our heart by thinking on it!) 149) I know You hear my cry according to Your loving kindness. Lord, You revive me according to Your judgment. 150) The wicked draw near. They are far from Your laws. 151) Yet <u>You Oh Lord are near to those who cry out for Your help</u>. All Your commandments are truth. 152) <u>You have established Your testimonies and they will forever be our foundation!</u>"

<u>Stage 2: Pupa</u> (he goes into a state of seclusion) So you will **rewrite the Scripture in your own handwriting.** Then meditate a few minutes on the meaning of these wonderful scriptures. This is important to help get the Word into your heart.

<u>Stage 3: Butterfly</u> (Maturity comes about as you <u>let the Word work in you.</u>) **Read, pray, or sing these verses out loud two or three times to God.** Verse 149 tells us why God hears our cries. It is not because we are 'good Christians'. No matter what your child does, when they are in trouble, you come to their rescue simply because your heart adores them. So it is with God and those who are His. He hears our cries and His heart is full of loving kindness for us. Sometimes He may have to correct us, but His heart is still full of love for us. So God hears our cries because He has tender mercy for us. It is such a good assurance to know He hears us because He is good! Verse 151 affirms He is near to those who cry out for help. Let us help ourselves by being innocent in any matter that we cry out to God about so it will be an easier defense. Since God is just, if we cry out to Him concerning something we are equally guilty about, then we will receive correction in that matter along with the other

person we are going to God about. But we can rest assured He will come to us for He has said in His Word that 'He is near to those who cry out to Him'. Because God is loving kindness we can be assured He will never turn His back on His children. Sometimes He has to discipline us; but that is not rejection. A person who is not secure in God's love for them may not know that discipline is not rejection. It is just the opposite. Hebrews 12:6 shows us that the proper correction is love. "(They) whom the Lord loves He corrects; and He disciplines every son (child) whom He receives." Everyone who becomes His; God will direct, correct as any parent would, and discipline because he is His child. **Knowing that God loves you is vital in your relationship with Him. Open your heart today and allow Him to show you.** Let His Love for you be your focus today.

Journal notes:

DAY 118

Stage 1: Caterpillar (remember he devours much food in preparation) First, read the Scripture to yourself.

Psalms 119:153-160 RESH "Lord, You have considered my affliction and delivered me; for I do not forget Your laws (Word). 154) You are my defense. You deliver me. You revive me according to Your Word. 155) Salvation is far from the wicked because they do not seek Your Ways, Your Word, Your Face. They do not love You at all. 156) Yet Great are Your tender mercies Oh God. You revive me according to Your judgments. 157) I do not decline from Your testimonies although my persecutors are many. 158) I saw the wicked sinning, and it grieved me; because they do not love (You) nor keep Your Word. 159) Oh Lord, I love Your precepts (rules for moral conduct). Revive me Oh Lord according to Your loving kindness. 160) Your Word is truth and has been from the very beginning. Every one of Your righteous judgments endures and is forever!"

Stage 2: Pupa (he goes into a state of seclusion) So you will **rewrite the Scripture in your own handwriting.** Then meditate a few minutes on the meaning of these wonderful scriptures. This is important to help get the Word into your heart.

Stage 3: Butterfly (Maturity comes about as you <u>let the Word work in you.</u>) **Read, pray, or sing these verses out loud two or three times to God.** Praise is not just for when you are happy. In fact, it is the most powerful if **<u>when you are coming against a hard time</u>** you **<u>open your mouth and praise!</u>** Praising when your heart is broken, or you have a great need, surrounds you with the Glory and the Presence of Almighty God! It begins the healing process in your heart. It is vital if you are to walk out of that situation victorious. Grumbling, complaining or keeping your mouth shut and holding praise in is just what the devil wants because it cripples you in the heat of the battle. Praise God even if you don't feel like it until you do! The grumbler is overcome. **<u>The praiser is an overcomer.</u>** I have learned a great deal about God's faithfulness through this Praise Devotional. When my son was 8, his father died. When

we sat him down and told him, he cried. Then about an hour later, he was taking his bath before bedtime and we heard him in there singing praises to God. It touched me because *in the midst of my son's grief, he was praising God*! The amazing part is that one year before that, my son was born again. When he was, he began praying in earnest for his father's salvation. Within a few months, his father became born again! Satan lost the battle for his soul, so I believe it was fitting for my son to sing praises to God even in the midst of his grief. In the Garden of Eden, Satan convinced Eve that God was not as good as He appeared. We cannot fall for that same lie! It is vital for us to keep our focus on God's goodness, and His faithfulness in these days. Praise helps us do just that and win major victories! So open your mouth NOW and praise God aloud. The victory is in your mouth as you praise God aloud with the Word! Let this be your focus today: take the Scripture that speaks the most to you today and speak it all day long.

Journal notes:

DAY 119

Stage 1: Caterpillar (remember he devours much food in preparation) First, read the Scripture to yourself.

Psalms 119:161-168 SCHIN "Even though I am persecuted unjustly; yet I will stand in awe of (and believe) Your Word. 162) My heart rejoices in Your Word, as one who finds a thing of great worth and value. 163) I detest lying, but I love Your law. 164) **Seven times a day do I praise You,** even more because You are a Righteous Judge. 165) They who love Your law have great peace! Nothing shall offend them. 166) Lord, my hope is in Your salvation and I (shall) keep Your commandments. 167) My soul has kept Your testimonies. I love them exceedingly. 168) I have kept Your precepts and Your testimonies. All my ways are before Your eyes!"

Stage 2: Pupa (he goes into a state of seclusion) So you will **rewrite the Scripture in your own handwriting.** Then meditate a few minutes on the meaning of these wonderful scriptures. This is important to help get the Word into your heart.

Stage 3: Butterfly (Maturity comes about as you <u>let the Word work in you.</u>) **Read, pray, or sing these verses out loud two or three times to God.** We should always be in awe of God. I look at His creation and I am awed. I look at the complexity of the human body and I am awed. His work is magnificent! Verse 164 shows us we should keep praise on our lips and in our heart all day long. If we don't focus on praise, we tend to fall into grumbling like the unbelievers around us. Be in awe of God continually. This keeps your heart tender toward Him. **Praise has to become part of who you are.** Praise brings us into victory! Let this be your focus today: take the Scripture that speaks the most to you today and speak it all day long.

Journal notes:

DAY 120

Stage 1: Caterpillar (remember he devours much food in preparation) First, read the Scripture to yourself.

Psalms 119: 169-176 TAU "Thank You Lord that You always hear my plea; and You give me understanding according to Your Word. 170) Lord, my supplication (request) comes up before Your throne. You deliver me according to Your Word, O Lord! 171) My mouth shall utter praises to You forever; for You teach me Your statutes. 172) <u>My tongue shall speak</u> of <u>Your Word</u>; for all Your commandments are Righteous. 173) I know Your Hand upholds me, for I have chosen Your precepts (and Your ways). 174) I have longed for Your salvation, Oh Lord. Your law is my delight. 175) As my soul lives, so shall I praise You, Oh Lord. Your judgments help me. 176) When I have gone astray, You sought me; and I do not forget Your commandments Oh God!"

Stage 2: Pupa (he goes into a state of seclusion) So you will **rewrite the Scripture in your own handwriting.** Then meditate a few minutes on the meaning of these wonderful scriptures. This is important to help get the Word into your heart.

Stage 3: Butterfly (Maturity comes about as you <u>let the Word work in you.</u>) **Read, pray, or sing these verses out loud two or three times to God.** We cannot even imagine right now the joy and the praises in heaven. The beginning of joy is to be born again. Then joy continues as we reverence God in our heart, and praise Him continually with our mouth. Many Scriptures talk about the praises that come from the earth. God is so awesome that if we the highest form of His creation, do not praise Him, the rocks will cry out in praise! In Luke 19, for example, when Jesus rode into Jerusalem just before His crucifixion, the people were praising Him. The Pharisees (religious leaders of that day) spoke to Him to shut the people up. Jesus' answer to them in verse 40 was: 'I tell you that if these (people) hold their peace (voice, and do not praise Me), the stones would immediately cry out!' God is very much due praise! The earth was created to glorify Him. If we do not, the earth itself will because **God is due great praise. God is magnificent, glorious, mighty and Holy. He alone is God!** Something magnificent happens not only in our hearts, but also in the earth when we lift up our voice and praise God! Praise God with all your might for He is worthy to be praised! **Spend some time this morning praising God. Then take that praise with you today!**

Journal notes:

DAY 121

Stage 1: Caterpillar (remember he devours much food in preparation) First, read the Scripture to yourself.

Psalms 120 "<u>In my distress, I always cry unto You Lord; and You always hear me!</u> 2) You always deliver my soul from lying lips and from a deceitful tongue. 3) What shall be the reward of the lying tongue? 4) The sharp arrows of the mighty will fall the lying tongue; with coals of fire the lying tongue will be set on fire! 5) Although I dwell near them (who are of a lying tongue), 6) yet my soul longs for peace. 7) I am for peace. (God be with me!)"

Stage 2: Pupa (he goes into a state of seclusion) So you will **rewrite the Scripture in your own handwriting.** Then meditate a few minutes on the meaning of these wonderful scriptures. This is important to help get the Word into your heart.

Stage 3: Butterfly (Maturity comes about as you <u>let the Word work in you.</u>) **Read, pray, or sing these verses out loud two or three times to God.** In verse 1 we see that God is the One to whom we are to cry to in times of distress. That is because He is the answer. Every time I am in distress, <u>I cry to You Lord</u>. And You hear me every time. You are not a God who is deaf to me. You are not a God who does not care! And You have never failed to deliver me from the wicked! In many cases the lying tongue (in verse 4) is the devil speaking into our mind. But the 'sharp arrows of the mighty' (the truth in the Word of God) will cause those lies of the devil to fall to the ground. We must know the truth (the Word). We must be assured of God's love for us personally; or else we will fall for the devil's lies. The truth is a sharp arrow. It causes lies to fail to produce despair. The truth produces hope in us. Hope gives joy. Joy gives strength and faith! My husband and I have a Book of Remembrance. In it we write specific times when God moved miraculously in our lives and there are quite a few stories in it. But the truth is, if we were to list all God does for us daily, we would never have room for all the written books. The same was said in the New Testament of Jesus' works when He walked on the earth; that there wouldn't be room to contain all the books in

this world to list all the miracles Jesus performed. That says to me that God is continually working on our behalf. I think it is time we started recognizing His Hand in our lives. He is always there. He gives us life every day; air to breathe. The list really is endless. **Spend some time this morning praising God.** And give God praise all day today for the big and the little things; for He is worthy to be praised!

Journal notes:

DAY 122

<u>Stage 1: Caterpillar</u> (remember he devours much food in preparation) First, read the Scripture to yourself.

Psalms 121 "I will lift up my eyes unto the hills from whence (where) my help comes. 2) My help comes from the Lord, who made heaven and earth. 3) He will not allow my foot to be moved. He that keeps me (safe) does not sleep (is always awake). 4) He who keeps Israel (in the palm of His Hand) neither sleeps nor slumbers (nor is absent in your need). 5) **<u>The Lord is my keeper (and my helper). The Lord covers me in all matters.</u>** 6) Neither will the sun overtake me by day; nor the moon by night. 7) The Lord preserves me from all evil. He preserves my soul from destruction. 8) The Lord preserves me when I go out and when I come in from this time forth and forever more!"

<u>Stage 2: Pupa</u> (he goes into a state of seclusion) So you will **rewrite the Scripture in your own handwriting.** Then meditate a few minutes on the meaning of these wonderful scriptures. This is important to help get the Word into your heart.

<u>Stage 3: Butterfly</u> (Maturity comes about as you <u>let the Word work in you.</u>) **Read, pray, or sing these verses out loud two or three times to God.** Repeat verse 5 out loud over and over and over until there is peace in your heart. **<u>Spend some time this morning praising God.</u>** Take this with you today in your heart; and when fear or a need arises, open your mouth and declare the Word of God! Job 22:28 says "You shall decree (declare) a matter, and it shall become an established fact, and the light will shine upon your ways!" What does that mean? In short it means if you speak a thing over and over and over, your soul will establish that thing to be in your life. This works in the good and the bad. In the Old Testament days, when a King made a decree, his word was absolute law; and whatever he said was carried out. A decree back then was made to come to pass because the one in authority said to make it happen. Well, we have the Holy Spirit in us (as born again believers). Therefore now we are in authority on the earth under God's headship. If we decree a matter, then the spirit realm immediately goes about to bring it to pass. But the same way a seed in the ground takes time to grow, so our words take time. So when your heart is determined to bring the Word of God to pass in your life, you plant a seed by speaking it out loud. (You also plant a seed in the natural. Example, if you need groceries, you give groceries to a needier person. If you need mercy, you give mercy. Plant a seed in the natural as well as in the spiritual realm. Don't limit your seed planting to just these two examples.) You water that seed daily so it can grow by continually speaking it. Then in the right time when the seed is full grown, it will manifest in your life. That is why it is so important for us to learn to **speak God's Word continually** and not the devil's words. Let's decree all day long today that Psalm 121 be established to us. Decree it over yourself. Decree it over your family, your spouse, your children and grandchildren. And praise God as you decree it!

Journal notes:

DAY 123

Stage 1: Caterpillar (remember he devours much food in preparation) First, read the Scripture to yourself.

Psalms 122 "I was (so) glad when they said unto me, let us go unto the house of the Lord. (For I love Your Presence Oh Lord. I love to be with You! You are mighty. You are holy. You are my God!) 2) Our feet shall stand within the gates of the holy city Jerusalem! 3) Jerusalem is the city of God, 4) where all nations go up to give thanks to the Name of the Lord, our Lord! 5) For there in it are thrones of justice. 6) So I pray for the peace of Jerusalem. All who love Jerusalem shall prosper. 7) Peace is within your walls oh Jerusalem. Prosperity is within your palaces. 8) Peace to you oh Jerusalem. 9) The house of God is there. I seek the good of Jerusalem!"

Stage 2: Pupa (he goes into a state of seclusion) So you will **rewrite the Scripture in your own handwriting.** Then meditate a few minutes on the meaning of these wonderful scriptures. This is important to help get the Word into your heart.

Stage 3: Butterfly (Maturity comes about as you <u>let the Word work in you.</u>) **Read, pray, or sing these verses out loud two or three times to God.** Fasting increases your strength. Any time the Lord tells you to fast, obey right away. I fasted 21 days at the beginning of these 150 days of praise; and revelation was increased unto me as to what to write. If there is one stubborn obstacle you cannot get past with just prayer, double your strength with fasting. Triple it with continual praise! In Revelation 4 John is writing about a vision he saw of the throne room in heaven. In verse 8 he talks of **continual praise before the throne of God**. "And the four beasts each had 6 wings and they were full of eyes. And **they ceased not night or day but continually praised saying Holy, Holy, Holy Lord God Almighty, which was and is and is to come!**" Then in verse 10 it says the 24 elders fell down before the Lord and praised God. In verse 11 we see what they say: 11) "You Oh Lord are worthy to receive glory, honor and power. You have created all. For Your pleasure they are and were created!" If praise is continual in heaven; how much more should it be continually in the earth from us- His people?! Holy, Holy, Holy are You Lord God Almighty! Let this be your focus today: take the Scripture that speaks the most to you today and speak it all day long. The heavens truly open up when praise is heard on the earth!

Journal notes:

DAY 124

Stage 1: Caterpillar (remember he devours much food in preparation) First, read the Scripture to yourself.

Psalms 123 "Unto You Oh Lord do I lift up my eyes, for You dwell in the heavens. 2) In the same way that the servant looks unto their master, so our eyes look unto You, Oh Lord our God; for You have mercy on us! 3) You have mercy on us; Oh Lord! You have mercy on us. We need You so. 4) The proud scorn us, the wicked harass us. (But we look unto You for mercy!)"

Stage 2: Pupa (he goes into a state of seclusion) So you will **rewrite the Scripture in your own handwriting.** Then meditate a few minutes on the meaning of these wonderful scriptures. This is important to help get the Word into your heart.

Stage 3: Butterfly (Maturity comes about as you <u>let the Word work in you.</u>) **Read, pray, or sing these verses out loud two or three times to God.** Until Jesus comes back, there will be injustice in this world. But our eyes are on God for we are as His servants who look to Him to make all things right again. I used to struggle to release my problems to God. Since I've been on these 150 days of praise, I find my confidence in God has grown immensely. **<u>I know I am His.</u>** And I know He takes care of what belongs to Him! **<u>Our part is to release that problem into His capable and loving Hands and trust Him to make all things right. There is nothing in this entire universe that He cannot make right again; or restore if we will trust Him to do so!</u>** Let this be your focus today: take the Scripture that speaks the most to you today and speak it all day long. Remember, Mercy is who He is!

Journal notes:

DAY 125

<u>Stage 1: Caterpillar</u> (remember he devours much food in preparation) First, read the Scripture to yourself.

Psalms 124 "If it had not been that You, Lord were on our side, 2) when our enemy rose up against us; 3) then we would have been swallowed up quick. 4) Lord, if You had not been on our side, then our troubles would have overtaken and overwhelmed us; 5) our soul would have drowned in despair. 6) But blessed and Holy is Your Name, Oh Lord, for <u>You keep us safely from the enemy</u>! 7) You give us a way to escape! You break the enemy's power so we can escape! 8) I declare that our help is in the Name of the Lord who made heaven and earth; for when we call on You, You are there!"

<u>Stage 2: Pupa</u> (he goes into a state of seclusion) So you will **rewrite the Scripture in your own handwriting.** Then meditate a few minutes on the meaning of these wonderful scriptures. This is important to help get the Word into your heart.

<u>Stage 3: Butterfly</u> (Maturity comes about as you <u>let the Word work in you.</u>) **Read, pray, or sing these verses out loud two or three times to God.** Victory comes quicker these days because I have learned the power of praise! I grumble less and praise God more. Joy is inside me more. I recognize grouchiness quicker and know how to get rid of it! Praise chases fear, anxiety and even anger away! Praise is saying fear is not your god, the Lord is God, and on the throne in your heart! Praise refreshes and restores you. Say these scriptures out loud over and over and over and over until joy bubbles up inside you; and you know God is on your side; and He has broken the enemy's power. He has given you an escape route! Let this be your focus today: take the Scripture that speaks the most to you today and speak it all day long.

Journal notes:

DAY 126

Stage 1: Caterpillar (remember he devours much food in preparation) First, read the Scripture to yourself.

Psalms 125 "Because I trust in You Lord, I will be as Mt Zion which cannot be moved), abiding forever. 2) Just as the mountains surround Jerusalem, so **you Lord surround Your people forever more**! 3) The anger of the wicked shall NOT strike the righteous; unless the righteous put forth themselves to sin. 4) Lord, you do good to/for those who are good, and upright toward You in their heart. 5) As for those who turn aside to wickedness, they shall be lead about by their sin, yet peace shall be upon Israel and the people of God!"

Stage 2: Pupa (he goes into a state of seclusion) So you will **rewrite the Scripture in your own handwriting.** Then meditate a few minutes on the meaning of these wonderful scriptures. This is important to help get the Word into your heart.

Stage 3: Butterfly (Maturity comes about as you <u>let the Word work in you.</u>) **Read, pray, or sing these verses out loud two or three times to God.** Following God truly is the best way. My heart forever falls in love with God! Verse 1 talks of trusting in God. Now I don't know about you, but there are a few areas in my life that are very dear to me; one being my children and grandchildren. Placing them in His Hands and fully trusting Him has been something I have been learning to do. When trust in Him is complete/full; you cannot be moved off of it by fear. You know deep within that Father God will not let you down. So you become stable - unshakeable in your faith. Your prayers are in faith, not fear; thus there is power in your prayers. James 5:16 "The effectual fervent prayer of a righteous person (godly person of faith) avails much (brings much results)!" Satan would love to move us off of our faith stand because when our trust wavers, our faith wavers. It is a shifting of trust from God to the lies Satan feeds you. Believing what you 'see' with your eyes will 'clog up' your ability to pray and see things change. Instead, choose to believe what God has said to you in His Word. Then you will have peace and can **pray in faith knowing God does love you and He is faithful.** He is surrounding you and protecting you just as verse 2 says. Just do not walk out of His protection barrier. Verse 3 shows that we are protected until we walk over the line into sin. <u>**When we have walked outside the protection barrier of God, we put ourselves in the territory of the enemy where we can get wounded.**</u> Let this be your focus today: take the Scripture that speaks the most to you today and speak it all day long.

Journal notes:

DAY 127

Stage 1: Caterpillar (remember he devours much food in preparation) First, read the Scripture to yourself.

Psalms 126 "Lord, because You have turned my captivity around, it is like a dream to me. 2) My heart is filled with laughter. Joy abounds. I am full of singing! We said in the ear of the unbeliever 'the Lord has done great things for us.' 3) The Lord has done great and marvelous things for us, for which we are so very thankful. 4) You Lord have turned around the things that once held us captive; and now evil flows away from us. (All generational curses have been broken!) 5) We sowed in tears, but we shall reap in great joy. 6) For he who goes forth and sows weeping bears a very precious seed. He shall without a doubt come again rejoicing; bringing in the harvest (rewards/fruit) of his work!"

Stage 2: Pupa (he goes into a state of seclusion) So you will **rewrite the Scripture in your own handwriting.** Then meditate a few minutes on the meaning of these wonderful scriptures. This is important to help get the Word into your heart.

Stage 3: Butterfly (Maturity comes about as you let the Word work in you.) **Read, pray, or sing these verses out loud two or three times to God. Spend some time this morning praising God.** You probably never knew God considers your tears precious whether they are tears of repentance or tears in prayer for another soul. In the natural realm, the most precious thing to the ground (soil) is rain. In the spirit realm, the tears of the righteous in prayer for the lost or for their brother/sister in Christ is also very precious and spiritually 'waters'. You know, even if all of your dreams haven't come to be yet, we are to still praise God for His infinite mercy towards us! A foundational characteristic of maturity is a thankful and a grateful heart along with humility. God has not called us to feel sorry for ourselves. He cannot use us that way; and nothing in our life will change if we insist on remaining in self-pity. Praising God brings great rewards. Praise Him BEFORE all your dreams come true! That is real faith and trust. Praise changes YOU so God can make all your dreams come true. Quit feeling sorry for yourself and focus on His goodness today. Tell Him all day long how lovely He is to you for He has indeed turned your captivity around through Christ Jesus!

Journal notes:

DAY 128

Stage 1: Caterpillar (remember he devours much food in preparation) First, read the Scripture to yourself.

Psalms 127 "Except the Lord builds the house, they are laboring in vain to build it. Except the Lord keeps the city, the watchmen waste their time to watch the city! 2) It is a waste for us to rise up early in worry; to sit up late fretting (in worry). For **God gives His beloved rest**! 3) Your children and grandchildren are an inheritance (a gift) to you from the Lord! The fruit of your womb is God's reward! 4) As arrows are (a delight) in the hand of the mighty hunter, so are the children of your youth! 5) Happy is the soul who has a peaceful home and is filled with his delight in his children. That home will have no shame, no regret and the father will be considered a leader in his community!"

Stage 2: Pupa (he goes into a state of seclusion) So you will **rewrite the Scripture in your own handwriting.** Then meditate a few minutes on the meaning of these wonderful scriptures. This is important to help get the Word into your heart.

Stage 3: Butterfly (Maturity comes about as you <u>let the Word work in you.</u>) **Read, pray, or sing these verses out loud two or three times to God. <u>Spend some time this morning praising God.</u>** Whatever it is that we want our life to be - it will not be a success unless we allow the Lord to build it and direct us! Anything we build will fall apart. Verses 1 and 2 show it is futile for us to try to do things ourselves. A man wants peace in his home; and respect in his community. Chapter 127 shows how to obtain it. Verse 1-Let God in. Let God build your life. **Let God** actually **be God**. Verse 2-Trust God. Do not let fret and worry in the door. If you do, they will take over and you will not sleep. Verse 3, 4-Appreciate the spouse and children God has given you. Your family is God's gift to you. Verse 5-Live your life in peace. Love your spouse and children second only to God. Then you will be satisfied, happy and fulfilled in life! Let this be your focus today: take the Scripture that speaks the most to you today and speak it all day long.

Journal notes:

DAY 129

<u>Stage 1: Caterpillar</u> (remember he devours much food in preparation) First, read the Scripture to yourself.

Psalms 128 "I am blessed because I fear/revere the Lord, my God. I have chosen to walk in His Ways! 2) I shall eat the labor of my hands (it will not be stolen from me). I shall be happy, blessed and at peace. It shall be well with me. 3) We shall bear healthy children like a vine bears much healthy fruit. Our children shall be around our table as an olive plant-flourishing and happy. 4) Behold, these are the blessings that shall be for any man who fears and reveres the Lord God Almighty! 5) The Lord God shall bless us out of the holy Mount Zion. We will see the goodness of Jerusalem all the days of our life. 6) We will see our grandchildren grow up and (we will see) peace upon Israel!"

<u>Stage 2: Pupa</u> (he goes into a state of seclusion) So you will **rewrite the Scripture in your own handwriting.** Then meditate a few minutes on the meaning of these wonderful scriptures. This is important to help get the Word into your heart.

<u>Stage 3: Butterfly</u> (Maturity comes about as you <u>let the Word work in you.</u>) **Read, pray, or sing these verses out loud two or three times to God.** Honestly, sometimes the pressures of this life press in on us so hard that we lose sight of just how much God does love us, bless us and take care of us. It is time we focused in on that, instead of our problems! It's kind of funny sometimes when we see ourselves from someone else's perspective. For instance, we sometimes feel sorry for ourselves, while others envy what we have. The bible says the angels are amazed seeing God's love for us. The wicked and the unbeliever have no peace and we have! **<u>God adores us.</u>** His every thought is upon you and me! We are the most unique and highly valued of all of God's creation. But do we always appreciate that? A tree is not created like Him! Jesus Christ did not die for a bunny, although very cute. He died for us; so we could have heaven and life! Even the angels cannot worship God the way we can. Our worship is very precious because God paid

a high cost for our redemption! All of this to say, we forget all the blessings God has heaped upon us. Like spoiled bratty children we just cry for more without really appreciating and seeing what we do have that He has given us. **A humble, pliable and grateful heart has a great deal of value in God's eyes.** And too often trouble comes to help us see our unthankful heart and attitude. Job is very famous in the bible for all the grief he suffered. In one day, all of his children died, his riches were gone and his health was taken away. Yet he refused to 'curse God and die'. He made a few mistakes, but he kept on trusting and believing God. If he could do it in the midst of his suffering, shouldn't we be able to in our tiny suffering (in comparison to Job's)? OK. Now you know the facts. But just knowing facts is useless unless you apply it to your heart! Remember today that trusting and praising God even in a trial brings us through the trial!

Journal notes:

DAY 130

Stage 1: Caterpillar (remember he devours much food in preparation) First, read the Scripture to yourself.

Psalms 129 "I praise Your Name God for though I have been afflicted many a time; 2) yet my enemy has never prevailed over me! 3) I praise Your Name Lord, for although trials of life have dug deep into my heart at times, 4) yet You Lord, my God are faithful to me! I praise Your Name Lord, for You have cut the enemies' cords that had me bound! 5) I praise Your Name Lord, for the enemy (that hates You and Your people) You have confused them and turned them backwards. 6) They are like grass that withers before it is grown up. 7) I praise Your Name Lord, for the wicked shall not prosper in their way! 8) Neither shall the blessing of the Lord be upon them. I praise Your Name Lord, for Your Name and Your blessings are upon us, Your people!"

Stage 2: Pupa (he goes into a state of seclusion) So you will **rewrite the Scripture in your own handwriting.** Then meditate a few minutes on the meaning of these wonderful scriptures. This is important to help get the Word into your heart.

Stage 3: Butterfly (Maturity comes about as you <u>let the Word work in you.</u>) **Read, pray, or sing these verses out loud two or three times to God.** Verse 6 says our enemy can be cut before they get a chance to take root. We are over -comers! God wants us to know it and walk in victory; not to feel defeated and walk in defeat. Our enemy can be cut down before it takes root in our life. We are like the grass in that God gives rain to the grass. Grass does not pray for rain to fall on it so it will live. God just takes care of the grass. Even more so, He cares about us. God pours His blessings out on us. He takes care of us without being asked to. A 6 month old doesn't have to ask to be fed. The mother cares about them and naturally takes care of their every need. So we are dependent upon God; and God cares about us. We are as dependant on God as the grass is. And God is faithful. If God is for us (and He is), then who can be against us? Let this be your focus today: take the Scripture that speaks the most to you today and speak it all day long.

Journal notes:

DAY 131

<u>Stage 1: Caterpillar</u> (remember he devours much food in preparation) First, read the Scripture to yourself.

Psalms 130 "Out of the depths of my sorrow Lord, I cried out to you. 2) And You have heard me. Your ear is very attentive to my voice in times of need, the way a mother's heart is attentive to her baby's cry. And You answer. 3) If we had to be sinless for You to hear, then who in all the earth would stand a chance? No one. 4) But with You there is great mercy and forgiveness. Because of it, You are revered. 5) My soul will wait on and trust in You alone. In Your Word is my hope placed. 6) My soul anticipates Your coming more than the night watchmen anticipate daybreak. 7) So let Your people Israel put their hope in You Lord. For with you there is mercy. With You Lord there is great redemptive power. 8) For You redeem Your people, Israel, from all bondage of sin!"

<u>Stage 2: Pupa</u> (he goes into a state of seclusion) So you will **rewrite the Scripture in your own handwriting.** Then meditate a few minutes on the meaning of these wonderful scriptures. This is important to help get the Word into your heart.

<u>Stage 3: Butterfly</u> (Maturity comes about as you <u>let the Word work in you.</u>) **Read, pray, or sing these verses out loud two or three times to God.** If we have ever doubted God's hearing ability, verse 2 settles it. And we should settle it in our heart. And what about verse 3? Verse 4 puts the icing on the cake. I think we've failed to see God's compassionate heart toward us even though John 3:16 has spelled it out for us. John 3:16 "**<u>For God so (deeply wanted and) loved</u>** the world (**<u>you</u>** and I), **<u>that He (made a way for reconciliation and) He gave (a valuable sacrifice of) His only begotten Son (for the very purpose</u>** of) **<u>so</u>** whoever (**<u>anyone who) believed in</u>** Him (**<u>Jesus) would not (have to) perish</u>** (in hell forever), **<u>but (could</u>** through believing on Jesus' sacrifice) **<u>have everlasting life (together in heaven with God</u>** for all eternity)!" If He didn't have compassion for us, He would have never sent Jesus to do what we could not-that is pay for our own sins. **If our sins are**

paid for (and they are), then there is NOTHING between us and God to prevent our relationship. You can shout here! NOTHING that is, except our wrong thinking. We think He is mad at us; or that He is untrustworthy; or that our sins are too horrible for Him to forgive. He has removed our sin so He could be close to us; and yet we run from Him! How dumb is that? Personalize John 3:16 by reading just the bold. Let this be your focus today.

Journal notes:

DAY 132

Stage 1: Caterpillar (remember he devours much food in preparation) First, read the Scripture to yourself.

Psalms 131: "Lord, You teach my heart humility; to not consider myself better than another; nor to consider myself smarter; nor to mind what is Your business. 2) You teach me to behave with gentleness and meekness, to know I have much to learn. You teach me to serve others in love. (For these are attitudes of good character.) 3) I will put my hope in You Lord, for You are my God. Let Israel put her hope in You!"

Psalms 132:7-9, 15 "We will go into the tabernacle (Presence) of the Lord. We will worship at His feet. 8) Arise, Oh Lord into Your rest; You and the ark of Your strength! 9) May Your priests be clothed with righteousness. Let all Your saints shout for joy! 15) Lord, You abundantly bless us with provision. You satisfy the poor with bread!"

Stage 2: Pupa (he goes into a state of seclusion) So you will **rewrite the Scripture in your own handwriting.** Then meditate a few minutes on the meaning of these wonderful scriptures. This is important to help get the Word into your heart.

Stage 3: Butterfly (Maturity comes about as you <u>let the Word work in you.</u>) **Read, pray, or sing these verses out loud two or three times to God.** We will focus today on the goodness of the Lord. We will shout for joy because God has clothed us with His Righteousness. Our God is a good God, full of mercy and truth! I am so humbled by what God has done in my life; and what He continues to do. **I will not let negative circumstances speak to me. I will meditate on the goodness of God; and the fullness of His Glory shall fall upon us!** God, You are so big, that the truth is, we do not have a worry in the world! Our children and grandchildren, our finances, our health and all relationships are in Your Hands. Our enemy is defeated! Isaiah 61:10-11 says: 10) "I will greatly rejoice in You Lord. My soul shall be joyful in You my God. For You have clothed me with the garments of salvation.

You have covered me with the robe of righteousness. I am as a bride adorned with jewels and a bridegroom decked out with the finest ornaments! 11) For as the earth brings forth a bud; as a garden causes the things sown in it to spring forth; so the Lord God causes righteousness and praise to spring forth in the sight of all nations!" Isaiah 61:3 says "God has appointed to those who mourn beauty to replace their grief, the oil of joy to replace mourning; and the garment of praise to replace the spirit of heaviness. And we will be called trees of righteousness planted by the Lord for His Glory!" Let this be your focus today: take the Scripture that speaks the most to you today and speak it all day long.

Journal notes:

DAY 133

<u>Stage 1: Caterpillar</u> (remember he devours much food in preparation) First, read the Scripture to yourself.

Psalms 133 "Behold, how good and how pleasant it is for brethren to dwell together in unity. 2) It is like the precious ointment upon the head. The anointing oil (which was poured on Aaron, the priest's head) flowed to the very bottom of his garments. 3) **The anointing and the Glory of the Holy Spirit covers (us) like dew covers the mountain! The Lord has commanded the blessing to be upon you;** and given you life forevermore!"

<u>Stage 2: Pupa</u> (he goes into a state of seclusion) So you will **rewrite the Scripture in your own handwriting.** Then meditate a few minutes on the meaning of these wonderful scriptures. This is important to help get the Word into your heart.

<u>Stage 3: Butterfly</u> (Maturity comes about as you <u>let the Word work in you.</u>) **Read, pray, or sing these verses out loud two or three times to God.** Since we are priests of God, this anointing is poured upon our head, flows over our shoulders and covers us with His Holy Spirit even down to our feet. The Holy Spirit covers us entirely so that God's Glory may cover, be upon us. Glory to God! Let this reminder be your focus today.

Journal notes:

DAY 134

Stage 1: Caterpillar (remember he devours much food in preparation) First, read the Scripture to yourself.

Psalms 134: "Behold, we praise You Lord for we are servants of the Most High God. 2) We lift our hands in Your sanctuary; and we praise Your Name! 3) For You are the Lord who made heaven and earth; and we give You the Praise in Zion!"

Psalms 135:1-6 "Lord, we praise You. We praise Your Holy Name. 2) We stand in Your House. In Your Courts we give You the praise due Your Name. 3) We praise You Lord, for You are good. We sing praises to Your Holy Name for Your Name is beautiful! 4) You have chosen Israel for Your very own. They are Your treasure. 5) I know that You are great and mighty. You are above all gods. 6) Whatever You pleased, You made in heaven and earth; in all the seas and the depths inside the earth."

Stage 2: Pupa (he goes into a state of seclusion) So you will **rewrite the Scripture in your own handwriting.** Then meditate a few minutes on the meaning of these wonderful scriptures. This is important to help get the Word into your heart.

Stage 3: Butterfly (Maturity comes about as you let the Word work in you.) **Read, pray, or sing these verses out loud two or three times to God.** There is no God like our God! Praise God over and over out loud with your mouth. Something beautiful takes place in our mind and heart when we just praise Him! His Presence covers us and His Glory falls upon us. Real praise comes from a heart that loves God. In I Chronicles 29:11-13 King David gave praise to God publicly. 11) "Yours, Oh Lord, is the greatness and power, the glory, the victory and the majesty. For all that is in heaven and earth is Yours. Yours is the Kingdom, Oh Lord. You are exalted as head above all. 12) Both riches and honor come from You. You reign over all. In Your Hand is power and might. It is in Your Hand to make great and to give strength to all. 13) Therefore God, we thank You. And we praise Your Glorious Name!" You see, God must be exalted in our hearts; then praised out loud with our mouth. For if praise is stuffed inside, it will die; and our heart will turn cold! So let us give Him the Praise He is due - out loud with our mouth! Psalms 24:7 calls Him the King of glory! Psalms 29:3 says He is the God of glory! Psalm 73:24 refers to heaven as the place of glory when the psalmist says "and afterward You will receive me into glory!" Psalms 85:9 shows that His glory can be upon us, and we should in fact desire it! Psalms 106 reveals that glory is due to God and God alone! Proverbs 25:27 shows glory does not come from us. Therefore God is the source of all beauty and glory! Isaiah 2:10 talks of God's glory being so amazing we cannot bear to look upon it. We are but dust. He is God and our God! **<u>Spend some time this morning and all day praising God for who He is.</u>**

Journal notes:

DAY 135

<u>Stage 1: Caterpillar</u> (remember he devours much food in preparation) First, read the Scripture to yourself.

Psalms 135:7-21 "Lord, You are all powerful. You cause vapors to come up from all over the earth. You make lightning for the rain. You brought the great winds out of Your many treasures. 8) When Your people were held captive in Egypt, it was You who smote the first born to make them let Your people go. 9) You sent many signs and wonders among the heathen with the 10 plagues. You did this for Your people Israel. 10) You protected Israel from many evil kings who came against them. 11) Many mighty kings more powerful than Israel were slain for Israel's protection. 12) And You gave Israel the land of their enemy as their possession forever. 13) Your Name Oh Lord endures forever. So is the memorial of all You have done for us. We will pass down the memorial of Your faithfulness to all generations (to our children and their children and their children). <u>We will forever talk of Your faithfulness and Your mercy, Oh God.</u> 14) For You alone are God! And You forgive us. 15) The wicked have gods made by their own hands. 16) They have mouths that cannot speak. They have eyes that cannot see. 17) They have ears and cannot hear their pleas. They simply are not alive. 18) So are all who put their trust in a block of stone (or wood). 19) But we praise You Lord! 20) We revere and praise Your Holy Name (for You are faithful)! 21) Praise be to our God who dwells among us. (You are alive! You have eyes to see, ears to hear our pleas and a mouth to speak. Your arm is strong to save Your people!) Bless the Lord!"

<u>Stage 2: Pupa</u> (he goes into a state of seclusion) So you will **rewrite the Scripture in your own handwriting.** Then meditate a few minutes on the meaning of these wonderful scriptures. This is important to help get the Word into your heart.

Stage 3: Butterfly (Maturity comes about as you <u>let the Word work in you.</u>)
Read, pray, or sing these verses out loud two or three times to God. Today sing these verses out loud. Sing praises unto the Lord for all He has done for you. Remind yourself all day of God's faithfulness!

Journal notes:

DAY 136

Stage 1: Caterpillar (remember he devours much food in preparation) First, read the Scripture to yourself.

Psalms 136:1-18, 21-26 "Oh I give thanks unto You Lord, for You are good. <u>Your mercy endures forever!</u> 2) Oh, I give thanks to the God of gods. For <u>Your mercy endures forever!</u> 3) Oh, I give thanks to You Lord for You are the Lord of lords. And <u>Your mercy endures forever!</u> 4) To You who alone (only) can do great and wondrous things. For <u>Your mercy endures forever!</u> 5) By Your wisdom the heavens were made. For <u>Your mercy endures forever!</u> 6) You stretched out the earth in the skies. And <u>Your mercy endures forever!</u> 7) You made the great lights. For <u>Your mercy endures forever!</u> 8) You made the sun to rule by day. For <u>Your mercy endures forever!</u> 9) You made the moon and the stars to rule by night. For <u>Your mercy endures forever!</u> 10) You smote Israel's enemy -the Egyptian in their first born. For <u>Your mercy endures forever!</u> 11) You brought Your people - Israel - out of bondage. For <u>Your mercy endures forever!</u> 12) With Your mighty hand and outstretched arm You saved Your people. For <u>Your mercy endures forever!</u> 13) You caused the Red Sea to part leaving dry land. For <u>Your mercy endures forever!</u> 14) You led Your people through the Sea on dry ground. For <u>Your mercy endures forever!</u> 15) When the enemy gave chase; You overthrew them in the Sea. For <u>Your mercy endures forever!</u> 16) Then You led Your people through the wilderness and gave them food and water. This You did; for <u>Your mercy endures forever!</u> 17) You smote mighty kings who came against Your people. For <u>Your mercy endures forever!</u> 18) They were arrogant in their might. But everyone heard of Your might! For <u>Your mercy endures forever!</u> 21) You gave their land to Your people as an inheritance. Why? Because <u>Your mercy endures forever!</u> 22) This became the inheritance of Israel, who belongs to You. For <u>Your mercy endures forever!</u> 23) You remembered us in our frailty. For <u>Your mercy endures forever!</u> 24) You've redeemed us from our enemies! For <u>Your mercy endures forever!</u> 25) You provide food for all flesh. For <u>Your mercy endures forever!</u> 26) Oh, we give thanks unto You God. For <u>Your mercy endures forever and ever! For Your mercy endures forever!</u>"

Stage 2: Pupa (he goes into a state of seclusion) So you will **rewrite the Scripture in your own handwriting.** Then meditate a few minutes on the meaning of these wonderful scriptures. This is important to help get the Word into your heart.

Stage 3: Butterfly (Maturity comes about as you let the Word work in you.) **Read, pray, or sing these verses out loud two or three times to God.** Go back through and read every 'for Your mercy endures forever'. There is a reason why this is repeated in this chapter again and again. God is telling us of His infinite mercy over us. **Think today of the many ways God has shown you His mercy and recite aloud all day that His mercy endures forever over you!**

Journal notes:

DAY 137

Stage 1: Caterpillar (remember he devours much food in preparation) First, read the Scripture to yourself.

Psalms 137 "By the rivers of Babylon, (when we were held captive by sin), we sat down and wept; for we remembered how good it was when the Lord was our keeper. (We remembered Psalm 23 that He was our shepherd who watched over us at night, and gave us food and guidance by day.) 2) We just cannot sing for joy in the midst of our trouble. 3) Our enemy has overtaken us. They mock us. (They think You have left us. But You will have mercy and bring us back unto You!) 4) Will we be able to sing to the Lord in the midst of our troubles? 5) We could never forget our Lord, our Savior, (although we did forget for a short while when we sinned). 6) But now repentance takes hold of our heart and God is our true love, our delight. (We see the error of our ways and turn back unto You God!) 7) Remember Lord, that we are Your children. Bring us back to our level of freedom and healing in You that we enjoyed before we strayed. 8) Our enemies are defeated! God's Arm has crushed Satan's head and released us from his clutches. (Great and Mighty are You God, for Your mercy on us endures forever!)"

Stage 2: Pupa (he goes into a state of seclusion) So you will **rewrite the Scripture in your own handwriting.** Then meditate a few minutes on the meaning of these wonderful scriptures. This is important to help get the Word into your heart.

Stage 3: Butterfly (Maturity comes about as you <u>let the Word work in you.</u>) **Read, pray, or sing these verses out loud two or three times to God.** We see in the scriptures that God's people turned from Him and got into sin quite a lot; and it got them into a lot of trouble. But when true repentance was in their heart, and they cried out to God; God always came to their rescue. He always delivered them from their enemies because of His great mercy. God does not condone sin. And often we face the consequences of our sins. But then He picks us up in His arms like a child and woos us back to Himself. He is the greatest Father there ever was because He NEVER stops loving us!

That kind of love just doesn't come from people. Only God can love us that way because He is love! It has been my experience (and is my opinion) that every time we get away from God it is because we are seeking something. And it gets us into trouble. When all the while, all we had to do was just get closer to God to find fulfillment! **God is all we need!** <u>**Sing a song of love to God from your heart today because He has never forsaken you.**</u>

Journal notes:

DAY 138

Stage 1: Caterpillar (remember he devours much food in preparation) First, read the Scripture to yourself.

Psalms 138 "I will praise You with my whole heart! Before the gods I will sing praises unto You! 2) I will worship with my face toward Your Holy temple. I will praise Your Name because of Your loving kindness and Your truth to us! You have magnified Your Word above all Your Name! 3) In the day when I cried, You answered me. And You gave me strength in my soul! 4) All the kings of the earth shall praise You oh Lord when they hear the Words of Your mouth. 5) They shall sing of Your ways; for great is the glory of the Lord! 6) Though You are God Almighty; yet You know (give attention to) and care about every lowly person. But the proud are far off from You God. 7) Though I may have trouble in my life, You revive me. You stretch forth Your Hand against my enemy; for Your Right Hand shall save me! 8) **You will bring into completion and perfect all matters which concern me!** Lord, Your mercy endures forever! I thank You Lord that You do not forsake the works of Your own Hands!"

Stage 2: Pupa (he goes into a state of seclusion) So you will **rewrite the Scripture in your own handwriting.** Then meditate a few minutes on the meaning of these wonderful scriptures. This is important to help get the Word into your heart.

Stage 3: Butterfly (Maturity comes about as you <u>let the Word work in you.</u>) **Read, pray, or sing these verses out loud two or three times to God.** Spend some time this morning praising God. These are mighty promises! According to verse 8, God can correct any situation that you face in your life. Many times I have quoted this verse in order to bring my heart in line with God so He could correct any area or situation that was out of line with His good Will for me. You can too! **<u>Sing verses 7-8 all day.</u>**

Journal notes:

DAY 139

Stage 1: Caterpillar (remember he devours much food in preparation) First, read the Scripture to yourself.

Psalms 139 "Oh Lord, You search me inside and out; and You know me. 2) You know all there is to know about me. You know and understand even my thoughts (and motives). 3) You cover me and surround me in my every step! You are even there when I'm asleep! You are very familiar with everything concerning me! 4) You know every word that I will speak. 5) You have covered (protected and anointed) me with Your Hand. You are behind me; and before me (to the left and to the right of me)! (For this I am so grateful!) Your Hand is upon my life! (You have declared that I am Yours!) 6) I am so in awe of You. I cannot comprehend all there is to know about You. 7) If I were to run from Your Presence; where could I go that You are not? 8) If I ascend into heaven, You are there. If I descend to hell, You can still reach me there! (No matter what predicament I am in, You can still save me and restore me!) 9) If I take the wings of the morning and dwell in the uttermost ends of the sea, 10) even there shall Your Hand lead me; Your Right Hand is still able to uphold me (to keep me from falling)! (Your faithfulness amazes me and is beyond my comprehension!) 11) When I feel like the darkness will swallow me up, 12) yet my darkness is not a problem for You! You shine Your light into my darkness and turn my night into day! 13) **My heart is given to You.** Even when I was in my mother's womb, You cared for and protected me (with a love beyond my ability to earn or repay). 14) I will forever praise You for I am fearfully (magnificently, marvelously) and wonderfully made! Marvelous (and amazing) are all Your works Oh Lord! 15) (You saw me and knew me), even in the innermost secret places of my mother's womb while I was being formed. 16) You watched my development. In fact You saw it before it actually was! 17) Your very thoughts are precious and sweetness to me, Oh God. 18) They are more than can be numbered! 19) God, You are my defense against the wicked who seek to slay me! 20) Their tongue is ever speaking against You Oh God. 21) I hate what You hate Lord. 22) I count Your enemies as my enemies. 23) <u>Search my heart, Oh God and know me.</u> Every thought is open to Your subjection. 24) If there be any wicked way in me, cleanse me Oh God and lead me in the way of eternal life! (You are my desire O God!)"

Stage 2: Pupa (he goes into a state of seclusion) So you will **rewrite the Scripture in your own handwriting.** Then meditate a few minutes on the meaning of these wonderful scriptures. This is important to help get the Word into your heart.

Stage 3: Butterfly (Maturity comes about as you <u>let the Word work in you.</u>) **Read, pray, or sing these verses out loud two or three times to God.** Spend some time this morning praising God. Open your heart more to God today. Remember God can remove all darkness. Sing this from verse 12 all day: You shine Your light into my darkness. And You turn my night into day!

Journal notes:

DAY 140

Stage 1: Caterpillar (remember he devours much food in preparation) First, read the Scripture to yourself.

Psalms 140 "Thank You, Lord, for you deliver me from the evil ones. You preserve me from the violent! 2) They may plot and plan evil in their hearts; and continually war 3) with poison and deceit in their mouth. 4) Yet You preserve me Oh Lord from their hands! <u>You preserve me and keep my family safe from the violent.</u> Though evil plots against us, yet You keep us safe! 5) The proud and arrogant plot to trap me. 6) But I said unto You Oh Lord that You are my God. You hear the voice of my cries. 7) You are God, the Lord, my strength and my salvation. <u>You cover my head with protection in the day of battle.</u> 8) You will not grant the wicked to overpower me. You will not permit the wicked devices to succeed over me! 9) Let the evil they have plotted fall back on their own head! 10) Cause their plans to fail and never rise again! 11) Do not let evil curses be established against Your people, O Lord! Let evil fall upon itself! 12) I know that You will maintain my cause! 13) <u>Let the righteous rejoice and give thanks unto your most Holy Name!</u> The upright shall glory and dwell in Your Presence!"

Stage 2: Pupa (he goes into a state of seclusion) So you will **rewrite the Scripture in your own handwriting.** Then meditate a few minutes on the meaning of these wonderful scriptures. This is important to help get the Word into your heart.

Stage 3: Butterfly (Maturity comes about as you <u>let the Word work in you.</u>) **Read, pray, or sing these verses out loud two or three times to God.** No one reading the Psalms could still say that God wants us to be defeated in this life. Spend some time this morning praising God and thanking Him for His continual protection over you and your family. Sing a song of love to God from your heart today and go forth into your day <u>knowing God wants you victorious</u>!

Journal notes:

DAY 141

Stage 1: Caterpillar (remember he devours much food in preparation) First, read the Scripture to yourself.

Psalms 141 "Lord, I cried unto You. You quickly answered my cry. (I know) when I cry out to You, You do hear my voice! 2) Let my prayer come before You as a sweet incense. <u>As I raise my hands to praise You, let it be a pleasing sacrifice to You! 3) Set a guard over my mouth, Lord to keep my lips from wrong.</u> 4) Teach my heart to do good and (to) resist evil. 5) When the righteous rebuke me and correct me, it is a kindness to me. It will not crush me, but it will help. It will be as anointing oil upon my head. 6) Evil will be overthrown, 7) and its remains scattered. 8) But my eyes Lord look unto You, my God; for in You I place my trust. I know You will not leave my soul destitute and without help! 9) You keep me from the snare evil has set for me. 10) Let wickedness fall into its own trap; while You cause me to escape!"

Stage 2: Pupa (he goes into a state of seclusion) So you will **rewrite the Scripture in your own handwriting.** Then meditate a few minutes on the meaning of these wonderful scriptures. This is important to help get the Word into your heart.

Stage 3: Butterfly (Maturity comes about as you <u>let the Word work in you.</u>) **Read, pray, or sing these verses out loud two or three times to God.** Notice verse 2 says let my prayer come before You (into the Presence of God) as a sweet incense (perfume). It does not say let my grumbling heart be my prayer! Praise and trust in God are as sweet perfume to Him. That is not saying we cannot come to God when our heart is broken and we need comfort or healing. That is saying grumbling is a bad spirit; and to do it habitually is displeasing to God. Praise honors God; therefore praise pleases God. But it does plenty for us too. **Praising God opens our heart** for healing, renewal and provision. **Praise is vital** for the victorious life we all want; but don't know how to obtain. The second sentence in verse 2 reveals that sometimes praise is a sacrifice because our heart is broken; and it is very difficult to praise God at that time. Yet that is when our praise is the most precious to God. And praising Him even in difficulty brings the victory we seek because it is saying 'I may not understand what is going on God, but I still trust You and I will follow You no matter what!' In verse 3 we see that we need God's strength to help us not to speak the wrong thing in difficult times. In verse 5 we see that sometimes God sends correction to us. Humility receives correction; but rebellion will not. Take a good look at your reaction when you are righteously corrected. Verse 5 also says correction has the effect of anointing oil on our head. Often oil in the bible represents a healing for you. Then in verse 7 we see victory over evil! So praise and the proper response to correction are connected to victory in our lives! Spend some time this morning praising God. Sing a song of love to God from your heart today.

Journal notes:

DAY 142

Stage 1: Caterpillar (remember he devours much food in preparation) First, read the Scripture to yourself.

Psalms 142 "I cried out unto You Lord with my voice. I made my supplication (request) unto You Lord. 2) I wept before You, telling You all my troubles. 3) My heart was overwhelmed within me. My enemies have laid a trap for me. 4) I looked all around me, and no one would help me. 5) So I cried out unto You, O Lord and **I declared and I said 'You are my refuge.** You are my (goodly) portion in the land of the living!' 6) For You hear my cry and You care. I was very low and You delivered me from my persecutors for their strength was more than mine. 7) You have brought my soul out of prison. I shall praise Your Name! The righteous shall join me in singing praises to You for You have (delivered me in all my troubles and You have) dealt bountifully with me!"

Stage 2: Pupa (he goes into a state of seclusion) So you will **rewrite the Scripture in your own handwriting.** Then meditate a few minutes on the meaning of these wonderful scriptures. This is important to help get the Word into your heart.

Stage 3: Butterfly (Maturity comes about as you let the Word work in you.) **Read, pray, or sing these verses out loud two or three times to God.** We can truly never say that we have delivered ourselves! God is our deliverer. In fact, God is our everything. Nothing is without Him! We mustn't wait until He has delivered us or done something for us, before we praise Him. He is God Almighty! That alone is reason enough to praise Him! Praise Him because He delivers you. But also praise Him just because He is God! In verse 5, **the psalmist took a stand in the midst of his troubles and made a declaration that God was his refuge!** Psalm 142 is like a story with a happy ending. He had grief and sorrow. But they weren't the final word. The story had a happy ending because God was his deliverer! And He is yours today! Remember that today as you declare aloud all day 'God, You are my refuge!'

Journal notes:

DAY 143

Stage 1: Caterpillar (remember he devours much food in preparation) First, read the Scripture to yourself.

Psalms 143 "(I am glad) You hear my prayer O Lord and You pay heed to my supplications (requests). In Your faithfulness (and Your Righteousness) You answer me! 2) You have given me mercy instead of the judgment (which I deserve); for in Your sight no man is justified within himself. 3) My enemy has come heavily against me persecuting me, endangering my life. I felt as if I were already dead. 4) I felt overwhelmed in my spirit and my heart was broken. 5) **Yet I keep my thoughts on Your goodness; Your faithfulness; and the mighty works of Your Hands (instead of focusing on my problems)!** 6) I bring my prayer request to You. My soul longs for You with a great thirst. 7) Lord, I know You hear me and I await Your answer. I know (You care and) You will not ignore me. I do not want to die without You! 8) Cause me to hear Your loving kindness early each morning Lord. In You I place my trust. Give me wisdom and understanding in the way I should go; for I look unto You for direction (guidance)! 9) You deliver me O Lord from my enemies. I run to You for defense. 10) Teach me Your Will, O Lord; for You are my God! Your Holy Spirit is good to me. You lead me into the way of uprightness. 11) Revive me O Lord, for Your Name's sake. For Your righteousness' sake, deliver me from trouble. 12) In Your mercy, cut off my enemies; for I am Yours!"

Stage 2: Pupa (he goes into a state of seclusion) So you will **rewrite the Scripture in your own handwriting.** Then meditate a few minutes on the meaning of these wonderful scriptures. This is important to help get the Word into your heart.

Stage 3: Butterfly (Maturity comes about as you <u>let the Word work in you.</u>) **Read, pray, or sing these verses out loud two or three times to God.** Remember Psalm 34:19? It says 'Many are the afflictions of the righteous, but the Lord delivers him out of them all!' Praise is a vital key to changing our heart. Then our circumstances can change. For me this has peeled back many layers of fear and reserve concerning God's love for me and His faithfulness to

my children. No longer is there doubt about whether He loves me or hears me, or will move on my behalf. My love for Him flows freely once again. Verses 1-5 of this Psalm first show the depth of trouble coming against the Psalmist. Then it shows a very deep secret to keeping your sanity and receiving victory in trials. Verse 5 says **'Yet (in the midst of my trouble) I (will choose to) keep my thoughts on God's goodness, God's faithfulness and the mighty works of His Hands!" Keeping praise in your mind, your heart and your mouth brings God on the scene in your behalf!** Practice that today.

Journal notes:

DAY 144

Stage 1: Caterpillar (remember he devours much food in preparation) First, read the Scripture to yourself.

Psalms 144 "Blessed are You Lord, my strength; for You teach me to battle (spiritually). 2) You are goodness to me; You are my fortress and my high tower (protection). You are my deliverer and my shield. You are the One in whom I trust. You subdue my enemy under me! 3) Lord, who am I that You (God) would take notice of me? 4) My time on earth is so short. 5) You bend the heavens Lord, and come down. The mountains will smoke at Your Presence Oh Lord! 6) You cast forth Your lightning and scatter my enemy. You shoot Your arrows and destroy my enemy. 7) You reach Your Hand from above and pick me out of my enemies' hands. (Hallelujah!) You deliver me from great overwhelming odds against me! 8) They are all liars and boasters. 9) But I will sing a new song to You, my God. I will sing praises unto You (for You are Beautiful)! 10) You give salvation unto (Your) kings. You have delivered me again and again. 11) You have delivered me from my enemy! 12) You have designed (purposed) that our sons may grow like strong plants (before You) and that our daughters would be polished cornerstones of a palace! 13) That our barns may be full of all kinds of wares. That our livelihood brings forth abundance! 14) That our work equipment be strong and never fail. 15) Happy are the people whose God is the Lord!"

Stage 2: Pupa (he goes into a state of seclusion) So you will **rewrite the Scripture in your own handwriting.** Then meditate a few minutes on the meaning of these wonderful scriptures. This is important to help get the Word into your heart.

Stage 3: Butterfly (Maturity comes about as you <u>let the Word work in you.</u>) **Read, pray, or sing these verses out loud two or three times to God. Praising God daily builds an intimate relationship with Him! Practice that today.**

Journal notes:

DAY 145

<u>Stage 1: Caterpillar</u> (remember he devours much food in preparation) First, read the Scripture to yourself.

Psalms 145 "I will exalt You, O God, my King. I will bless and praise Your Name forever! 2) Every day I will praise You Oh God. I will praise Your Name forever! 3) Great are You Lord; and greatly to be praised! Your greatness has no end! 4) Each generation shall praise Your mighty works to the next generation. (We shall tell our children. They in turn shall tell theirs. So on and so forth.) We shall openly declare Your mighty works to each other! 5) **I will talk about the Glory and the Honor of Your Majesty.** I will tell every one of Your wondrous works (toward me)! 6) And Your people shall speak of Your mighty acts (of deliverance for them). I will declare Your greatness. 7) We will abundantly talk of Your mighty goodness. We shall sing of Your Righteousness! 8) Lord, You are gracious and full of compassion (toward us). <u>You are slow to anger. You are full of great mercy!</u> 9) You are good to all people. Your tender mercies are over all the works of Your Hands. 10) All Your works shall praise You, O Lord. Your saints shall bless (and praise) You! 11) We will talk of the glory of Your Kingdom. We will talk of Your Power (and might)! 12) We will make known to our children Your mighty acts; and the glorious majesty of Your Kingdom! 13) For Your Kingdom is an everlasting Kingdom. Your Dominion is forever throughout all generations. 14) Lord, You uphold all who fall. You raise again those who are oppressed! 15) The eyes of Your people look to You for help. You give provision always right on time! 16) You open Your Hand and feed every living thing! 17) You are completely Righteous in all You do. You are Holy in all Your works! 18) Lord, thank You for You are always near to them who call upon You in sincerity and truth. 19) You will fulfill the desire of those who revere You in their heart! You hear their cry when they are needy; and You save! 20) Lord, You preserve all who love You; while the wicked are destroyed. 21) My tongue shall forever speak Your Praises. Let all flesh bless Your Holy Name forever and ever. Amen!"

Stage 2: Pupa (he goes into a state of seclusion) So you will **rewrite the Scripture in your own handwriting.** Then meditate a few minutes on the meaning of these wonderful scriptures. This is important to help get the Word into your heart.

Stage 3: Butterfly (Maturity comes about as you let the Word work in you.) **Read, pray, or sing these verses out loud two or three times to God.** Notice verses 1-7, 10-12 and verse 21 show us how much **we are to talk about God's goodness!** This gives you a concept of just how important it is to speak of God's faithfulness. Talk today about God's goodness!

Journal notes:

DAY 146

Stage 1: Caterpillar (remember he devours much food in preparation) First, read the Scripture to yourself.

Psalms 146 "Praise the Lord, oh my soul! I praise You Lord (for I know You love me)! 2) As long as I live, I will praise You Lord. I will sing praises unto You God while I have breath. 3) I will not put my trust in people (or money) for they are not my deliverer! 4) I do not place my trust in the creation; I place my trust in You God for You are the Creator! 5) Happy is the man who has God for his help! Happy is the man whose hope is placed in the Lord God! 6) For God is the maker of heaven and earth; the maker of the sea and all that is in it. Lord, You keep truth forever. 7) You give justice and bring justice for the oppressed! Lord, You give food to the hungry. **You loose the prisoners!** 8) You open the eyes of the blind - both physically and spiritually! God, You raise up those bowed over (both physically and spiritually)! You love the righteous! 9) God, You preserve the strangers. You relieve the fatherless and the widow. You turn upside down the ways of the wicked! 10) God You shall reign forever unto all generations. Praise the God of Zion!"

Stage 2: Pupa (he goes into a state of seclusion) So you will **rewrite the Scripture in your own handwriting.** Then meditate a few minutes on the meaning of these wonderful scriptures. This is important to help get the Word into your heart.

Stage 3: Butterfly (Maturity comes about as you let the Word work in you.) **Read, pray, or sing these verses out loud two or three times to God.** I love verse 7. God looses (frees) the prisoners! God gives us freedom from old hurts that still try to haunt us and from physical sickness. God gives us freedom from mental torment; even freedom from guilt and condemnation! God wants us free from all oppression of the devil! God provided it through Jesus on the cross! That is such a praise verse! Emotional and mental torment is the cruelest weapon Satan has. So many people today are bound up; breathing but not living the good life God planned for them. Hurts and wounds abound these days. Suicide and murder are very high on the death scale. Society does not know what to do. People need to be freed from their mental prisons. Hate, anger and rage are outward signs of mental and emotional turmoil. <u>Praise to God and forgiveness breaks all those chains</u> that Satan has tried to put on people. When thoughts of mental and emotional torment come, start singing praises to God. Satan will flee because he cannot stand praise. **Praise drives out every demon and every bondage. The demons cannot put bondage on you unless you let them.** Usually when we allow it, it is because we don't know we are letting it happen. For example, if someone hurts you, thoughts of anger come and offer themselves to you. If you do not resist them and ask God for help, those painful thoughts will remain and make a home in your mind and your heart. As the hurtful thoughts roll over and over in your mind (because you do not take God's Power to resist them); you are tormented. The longer they stay, the harder it is to get rid of them later. But if you resist Satan's offer right away and call on the Power of God for strength, then they MUST flee because God's Power (which you have called on) is greater than Satan's attempt to get you to accept his wickedness. When God's Power floods in, it washes away all the pain; and you can live again. God wants us to live and have a good life. <u>The one to whom we submit ourselves to is the one who will be our master.</u> Submission to God brings life and happiness; while submission to Satan brings death and destruction. James 4:7 says "submit yourselves therefore unto God; resist the devil and he will flee from you." Choose God and choose life! Determine today that you will be free from all oppression of the devil!

Journal notes:

DAY 147

<u>Stage 1: Caterpillar</u> (remember he devours much food in preparation) First, read the Scripture to yourself.

Psalms 147 "I praise You Lord. It is good for me to sing praises unto my God. It is pleasant and praise is comely (beautiful). 2) Lord, You build up Jerusalem and gather together the outcasts of Israel. 3) **You heal the broken hearted and bind up our wounds!** 4) You know the number of the stars and every one by their names. 5) How great You are Lord. How mighty is Your Power. Your understanding is infinite! 6) You lift up the meek and cast down the wicked. 7) I sing unto You Lord with thanksgiving. I sing praises unto my God! 8) For You God cover the heavens with clouds. You prepare rain to water the earth; and make grass to grow on the mountains. 9) You give food to all the animals. 10) Your delight is not in the strength of the horse; nor are You impressed by man's strength. 11) But **You are pleased with those who revere You; with those who put their hope in Your mercy.** 12) I praise You O Lord. Jerusalem rises to praise their God in Zion. 13) You strengthen the bars of the gates (that protect us). You have blessed us Your children within the gates of Jerusalem! 14) You make peace in Your borders; and fill our homes with the best. 15) You send forth Your commandment to the earth. Your Word runs quickly 16) to give snow (in its due time); 17) to give ice upon the earth. 18) You then send out Your Word again and the snow and ice melt. You cause the wind to blow and waters to flow (for us)! 19) You are faithful to show Your Word unto us; to teach us Your statutes and laws. 20) Your favor is upon Your people; as is Your justice. We praise Your Name, Lord!"

<u>Stage 2: Pupa</u> (he goes into a state of seclusion) So you will **rewrite the Scripture in your own handwriting.** Then meditate a few minutes on the meaning of these wonderful scriptures. This is important to help get the Word into your heart.

<u>Stage 3: Butterfly</u> (Maturity comes about as you <u>let the Word work in you.</u>) **Read, pray, or sing these verses out loud two or three times to God. As**

you read this out loud to God; let your spirit freely pour forth praises unto God for He is mighty! He is Holy! He is lovely and He is good! Let this be your focus today: take the Scripture that speaks the most to you today and speak it all day long.

Journal notes:

DAY 148

Stage 1: Caterpillar (remember he devours much food in preparation) First, read the Scripture to yourself.

Psalms 148 "I praise You, Lord. I praise You, Lord in the heavens. 2) All the angels praise You. All of the heavenly host praise You. 3) The sun, the moon and the stars praise You! 4) The whole universe gives glory to You Lord! 5) Let all that is praise the Name of the Lord. For You spoke and all was created! 6) You have established them to be forever and ever. You have decreed it; and it shall not pass away. 7) All in the seas praise You Lord. 8) Fire, hail, snow, vapor and stormy wind fulfill Your Word! 9) Mountains, hills, fruit trees 10) and all animals praise You! 11) Kings and all people 12) young and old alike, male and female, 13) **let all of creation praise Your Glorious Name. For Your Name is excellent above all.** Your Glory is above all things created. 14) You raise Your people up. Let the praise of all Your saints be lifted high. May Israel, Your dear (and beloved) one, be near You. We praise Your Mighty, Holy Name O Lord!"

Stage 2: Pupa (he goes into a state of seclusion) So you will **rewrite the Scripture in your own handwriting.** Then meditate a few minutes on the meaning of these wonderful scriptures. This is important to help get the Word into your heart.

Stage 3: Butterfly (Maturity comes about as you let the Word work in you.) **Read, pray, or sing these verses out loud two or three times to God.** The joy in praising God is so much better than the yucky feeling we get from grumbling, fear and hate! Spend time today praising God!

Journal notes:

DAY 149

Stage 1: Caterpillar (remember he devours much food in preparation) First, read the Scripture to yourself.

Psalms 149 "Father, God I praise You. I sing unto You Lord with a new song from my heart. I sing Your praises among Your saints. 2) Let Israel rejoice in You for You have made him. Let all the children of Zion be joyful in their King. (Let joy reign!) 3) Let us praise Your Holy Name as we dance before You! We sing praises with musical instruments! 4) You take pleasure in Your people. (The Lord delights in me. He is crazy about me!) You take joy in us! You cover the meek with the beauty of salvation.5) Let the saints be joyful in glory. Even on our beds in the morning and at night, let us sing and shout Your praises out loud! 6) **Let the high praises of our God be <u>continually</u> in our mouth;** and a two-edged sword in our hands! 7) For God brings vengeance on the unrighteous. 8) We bind the enemy with chains and their rulers are bound in iron! 9) Justice is executed upon them. This honor is given to all God's saints! Therefore all Ye His people, Praise the Lord!"

Stage 2: Pupa (he goes into a state of seclusion) So you will **rewrite the Scripture in your own handwriting.** Then meditate a few minutes on the meaning of these wonderful scriptures. This is important to help get the Word into your heart.

Stage 3: Butterfly (Maturity comes about as you <u>let the Word work in you.</u>) **Read, pray, or sing these verses out loud two or three times to God.** In a very big sense, praise ushers in the era of peace on earth because praise ushers in God's Presence. Yet also He is within every born again believer. So anytime you personally need peace, all you have to do is begin to praise God sincerely; and He and His peace will totally envelope (surround) you! Verse 3 shows us that dancing before the Lord is a good thing. It is very freeing. God isn't as interested in dignified as He is 'humble before Him'. Submission to God and confidence in God are all a part of worship as well as part of our daily relationship with Him. Real relationships have trust, transparency and

respect at their core. And that is what we should desire with God - a real relationship; not a phony baloney one. There is no joy, or fulfillment in phony relationships! Spend some time this morning praising God. Sing a song of love to God from your heart today. And dance!

Journal notes:

DAY 150!!!

Stage 1: Caterpillar (remember he devours much food in preparation) First, read the Scripture to yourself.

Psalms 150 "I come to Praise Your Name Lord. I praise, You, God for You are in Your sanctuary. I praise You God for the firmament of Your power! 2) I praise You God for Your mighty acts (of deliverance for Your people)! I praise You God according to your excellent greatness and majesty! 3) I praise You with the sound of the trumpet and all musical instruments. (Musical instruments were designed for praising God!) 4) I praise You with my dance before You; and with all stringed instruments as well. 5) I praise You with the loud cymbals. 6) **Let everything that has breath praise the Lord! Praise the Lord!**"

Stage 2: Pupa (he goes into a state of seclusion) So you will **rewrite the Scripture in your own handwriting.** Then meditate a few minutes on the meaning of these wonderful scriptures. This is important to help get the Word into your heart.

Stage 3: Butterfly (Maturity comes about as you <u>let the Word work in you.</u>) **Read, pray, or sing these verses out loud two or three times to God.** Verse 2 says two things to me. One is I praise God <u>because</u> of His excellent greatness and majesty. Two is I praise God according to (to the degree and measure of) His excellent greatness and majesty! Both recognize God's greatness and majesty. We should both praise Him <u>because</u> of it; and <u>to the degree</u> of it. His greatness and majesty are so high and deserve an equal amount of praise. The truth is our praise can never equal the degree of His excellent Glory and Worth. But if we strive for our praise to match His excellent Glory, we do well. And if we praise Him because of His excellent Glory, we do well! Really until we see Him 'face to face', we cannot even begin to comprehend His greatness. But we are to strive to with our praises to Him now. This may seem like an anti-climatic ending. But really, praising God should not be a chore. It should be a daily offering from us, His creation, to the Most Magnificent

and Glorious God and King! It is part of our love relationship with Him - a very important part! Selah. This is our final devotion together, but don't let it be your final praise!

Let praise be your lifestyle!

Journal notes:

CPSIA information can be obtained at www.ICGtesting.com
Printed in the USA
LVOW12s1226180914

404730LV00003B/4/P